warriors
witches
women

MYTHOLOGY'S FIERCEST FEMALES

Kate Hodges

ILLUSTRATED BY
HARRIET LEE-MERRION

WHITE LION
PUBLISHING

CHAPTER 1

WITCHES

Wise women, soothsayers and healers

CHAPTER 2

WARRIORS

Fighters, strategists and bringers of justice

CHAPTER 3

BRINGERS OF MISFORTUNE

Destructors, havoc-wreakers, harbingers of doom

CHAPTER 4

ELEMENTAL SPIRITS

Lightning bolt-throwers, commanders of fire and ice, creators of the planet

CHAPTER 5

MUNIFICENT SPIRITS

Bountiful deities, generous spirits, domestic goddesses

FOREWORD

Sometimes, the past can help us make sense of the now. Reading through the stories of the goddesses, witches and mythological creatures featured in *Warriors, Witches, Women*, I was struck by how present these women still are today. Sometimes their names are used as weapons – women in politics are called 'Medusa', women who speak their mind 'harpies' or women who wear make-up become 'Jezebels'. Entire groups are demonised. Women who have the power to heal, to care for others, who have skills in astronomy and herbalism or live on the fringes of society, have all been derided as 'witches' by those who would like to see their power and knowledge neutralised.

Women associated with strength – Artemis, Innana, Kālī, Morrígan and Mami Wata – are fierce influences, whose characters are so strong they endure down the years. So much so, these women are still referenced across popular culture – featuring in plays, TV shows, films, comic books and music videos. Reading about the origins of some of our most familiar characters is quite the eye-opener.

Then there are the less familiar tales – stories I'd never heard before. A quick dip into the book will throw up diverse narratives, from the volcanic rage of Hawaiian goddess Pele to the cheeky striptease of Ame-No-Uzume, while a deeper dive reveals arcs and connections across cultures, religions and continents. I also loved Harriet Lee-Merrion's illustrations, which bring the stories to life in cool, modern, intelligent style – capturing the imagination of every woman who has ever found herself in need of a powerful role model.

Maxine Peake

INTRODUCTION

'We are the granddaughters of the
witches you weren't able to burn.'

Goddesses, ghosts, witches, creatures. The mythological and fantastical have always fascinated me, but it was the female players who became an obsession. While my friends were mooning over Michael J. Fox and Tom Cruise, I was transfixed by *Clash of The Titans* (the 1981 version), where Perseus takes on various creatures to save Princess Andromeda. It wasn't hunky Harry Hamlin who seduced me, but the rickety figure of Medusa – stop motion artist Ray Harryhausen's snake-haired creature dragging herself around a fire-lit underground temple, eyes beaming green light. This sinister creature was far more fascinating than the vacuous stack of muscles which vanquished her. I was mesmerised. What was her story? What drove her? Why, even after death, did she retain her terrifying ability to turn all who gazed at her into stone? Most importantly, why did people have a *problem* with her?

Later came the witches. I was giddy over Helen Mirren as Morgana in the Arthurian epic *Excalibur* (1981), the chanting villagers from *The Children of the Stones* (1977), the White Witch from the Narnia tales, Fairuza Balk in *The Craft* (1996), the Wicked Witch of the West in *The Wizard of Oz* (1939), even the dodderingly sweet-but-evil Minnie Castevet in the cult *Rosemary's Baby* (1968). All these depictions were reductive and cartoonish in their different ways, but I'd still find myself rooting for these women. I loved their sense of self-possession, their knowledge, their power; they looked like they were having a lot more fun than the heroes and heroines who eventually defeated them.

I'd hoover up folk tales, from the Welsh *Mabinogion* with its tales of shimmering faerie princess Rhiannon to the Irish mythological cycles with the screaming warrior Morrígan. I'd spot seductively fascinating women in classical literature: the witches and sages Circe, Hecate, Cassandra and the bounding, athletic Artemis. I also devoured characters from further afield – the whirlwind fury of Kālī from Hindu tales, Anath from Semitic stories and the raging Pele from Hawaii. These are women who go beyond long-haired, smiling stereotypes, whose stories are so powerful, so entrancing that they have survived for *millennia*.

To a ten-year-old me, whose only female superhero was Wonder Woman, these mythological creatures resonated hard. They fought, took revenge, were wild – some of them were even worshipped for it. And it's their quirks, their power, their fallibility that makes them fascinatingly relevant to women today.

PICK AND MIX

Warriors, Witches, Women retells and reframes the incredible stories of some of these women. For space limitations, I've chosen to focus on fifty global entities, based purely on those whose stories resonate most deeply and reflect multiple experiences, from the mighty to the mundane. These are the mythological beings who have skills and character traits we can all aspire to, who are positive and strong and who, despite having a few millennia behind them, still feel modern and fresh. I've tried to tell the stories behind the blockbuster reworkings, to find the true origin tales and uncover how, and most importantly *why*, they have been retold again and again. To have these incredible creatures gathered together in one place is like a dream party, one where you might laugh with Freyja in her finery, snaffle crisps from the buffet with Futakuchi-onna, lift up your skirts and dance with Ame-no-Uzume and finish your night skinny-dipping with a selkie.

FIND YOUR TRIBE

I've grouped the stories into sections. First we find the *Witches*, wise women, soothsayers and healers. These are empowered women, many of whom deviated from the 'norm' and were cast as evil. Here we find Hecate, Baba Yaga and the icy Berchta making corporeal the fears of men, suspicious of knowledgeable women who might threaten the gender status quo.

Next come the *Warriors*, fighters, strategists and bringers of justice – women who don't just crush enemies, but battle expectations. Women like Yennenga, who are not just men's equals on the battlefield, but their betters. But they are not one trick ponies; they are nuanced, fallible.

In *Bringers of Misfortune* the focus is on the destructors, the havoc-wreakers and the harbingers of doom. These are the vengeful, the foreboding, the malignant women – the Harpies and Medusa among them – whose names are being reclaimed. They may be monsters, but they are *our* monsters.

Elemental Spirits hails the wild women – the lightning bolt throwers, commanders of the planet and those at one with the elements. The selkies, the Rainbow Serpent and Mari – these are the women who run free, cutting loose from the expectations and raised eyebrows of society. They lead the charge when our existence as a species is so horrifically under threat.

And finally there are the *Munificent Spirits*, the women it's easy to love. The bountiful deities, generous spirits and domestic goddesses. Maman Brigitte, the Moirae, Bona Dea –these are the women who put all others before themselves. Yet, all have a darker side, those fragments of reality we can identify with, which reflect back aspects of our humanity, and more specifically, *female* humanity.

There are many versions of each tale – in this sphere facts are fluid – so I've cherry-picked the most show-stopping. And I've tried my best to use language and names closest to those used by originators, but if I've muffed up, do let me know. This is a collaboration.

ALL IN THE TELLING

What I've enjoyed most about researching the book is uncovering just how these stories twist and change as they are passed from country to country and retold. As the unapologetically sexual Inanna's story spreads across the globe, she becomes Ishtar, the Hittite Sauska, and is echoed in Roman Venus and Greek Aphrodite. And the triple aspect maiden–mother–crone, spring–summer–winter figure epitomised by the Morrígan pops up across Europe and seeps into popular culture: you'll find her traces in the Greek Moirae, Norse Norns, the Celtric Matres and the Weird Sisters who foretell Macbeth's future.

Often, the telling is as much about the writers as it is their subjects; these women have been championed, snubbed and literally demonised in the name of politics, religion and the patriarchy. Goddesses who once reigned omnipotently could be pulled down by those who sought to replace what they represented with something more to their liking. However, these women's original characters still shine.

These names are whispered in bedtime stories across the world, standing the test of time and capturing the imagination of all people, regardless of gender, age or race. This language, and these archetypes and fables, form the bedrock of our culture and resonate with modern audiences, reworked by writers and filmmakers, playwrights and musicians (see my Mythological Women playlist, page 222). These figures don't purely provide a comforting link to history, but make for powerful contemporary role models, their struggles, hopes and strength resonating. These *fabulous* women may be from the darkest past, but they're leading the charge forward. And thank *goddesses* for that.

Kate Hodges

CHAPTER ONE

WITCHES

Wise women, soothsayers
and healers

HECATE

Also known as
Hekate

Perhaps, more than any other, Hecate lay down the blueprint for what is witch. Her sinister archetype has fascinated great minds down the centuries, entrancing writers such as William Shakespeare, William Blake and, more recently, the creators of the Marvel universe. This woman, with a penchant for wearing flowing, dark robes, roamed moonlit graveyards at the head of a pack of wild dogs. She also had a powerful knowledge of herbalism.

Hecate's distinctive look still appeals to those with a love for the dramatic; today, you're most likely to find her name posted as a 'witchspiration' hashtag on Insta-pagan social media accounts. However, dig a little deeper and you'll find much more. Hecate was a compassionate, clever woman dedicated to supporting her own gender at the most vulnerable times of their lives, as well as a defender of those living on the fringes of society.

Hecate's story is thought to have originated outside of Greece – in Thrace, Anatolia and even Egypt, where she may have had her origins in Heket, the frog-headed

god of midwifery. Her tale was carried in whispers to the Greeks, perhaps via the Sumerians and Israelites, who added some of their favourite demon Lilith's attributes (see pages 106–09), self-confidence and love of the night, to her character. By c. 700 BCE, she had been absorbed into the Grecian mythos, mentioned in Hesiod's *Theogony*, as a 'glorious goddess' who gave bounteous catches to fishermen, was a nurse to all living things, bestowed fertility and granted victories to her most favoured armies.

Hecate assumed a place in the pantheon of Greek Titan gods. This group of deities was, in time, vanquished by Zeus' Olympians in an epic battle to determine who ruled the universe. However, Hecate helped the Olympians during the war and so remained a goddess, honoured and respected by Zeus. Perhaps because of her origins outside the canon of original gods, she shunned the hubbub and intrigue of Mount Olympus, the home of the new breed of Olympian gods and goddesses, and chose to live alone.

At this point, Hecate was venerated as a generous spirit. She was a female-centric goddess, a guardian of households, her image found on domestic door pillars, rather than in huge temples. She was often depicted with a halo of stars and carrying two torches. This Hecate was the patron of midwives, healers helping with fertility and undertakers. She also protected newborns and boys on the cusp of manhood.

However, during the fifth century BCE, Hecate's reputation darkened. She became a chthonic goddess, most at home in the Underworld. Sophocles and Euripides associated her with death, sorcery and necromancy. It could be that these patriarchal writers, wary of Hecate's powerful reputation among women, demonised her, turning her into someone to be feared. The writers created an association between Hecate, her priestess, Medea, and the 'Thessalian women'. Those mortals were believed to have supernatural powers; they could 'draw down the moon from the sky' and were knowledgeable about herbs and remedies. In other words, they possessed the folk wisdom of women historically ascribed as 'witches'.

Hecate's torches now lit her way into shadowy, awkward places. She made a habit of making nocturnal expeditions to graveyards and empty streets, accompanied by ghosts, packs of barking dogs or sometimes the Furies (see pages 64–67). Despite these companions of the night – and her familiars, a black she-dog and a polecat, Hecate was a loner at heart. She was a virgin by choice and was never tied to a domestic life.

This Hecate was particularly associated with three-way crossroads, seen across cultures as places 'between worlds' where spirits lurk and souls linger (see the Cihuateteo, pages 68–71). People would leave offerings of cake and wine at these intersections and puppies were ritually sacrificed in her honour (dogs were sacred to Hecate. According to Virgil, their howling heralded her arrival). Triple-headed masks representing her face hung on poles at the junctions. It was perhaps because of this association that she began to be depicted as a triumvirate who could simultaneously divine the past, present and future, as well as commune with the dead.

An alternate theory is that she became triplicate after her most famous hour, when this 'tender-hearted' goddess helped Demeter find her daughter. Persephone had been betrayed by her father, Zeus, who allowed the god of the Underworld, Hades, to abduct his daughter and take her to his subterranean realms. The trio became close: Hecate was Persephone's confidante and accompanied her on her journeys back home to see her mother. Hecate was described in *The Orphic Hymns*, written in 300–200 BCE as 'the world's key-bearer never doom'd to fail', the one able to unlock the doors between this world and the next, the guide between life and death.

Hecate's dark reputation endured for millennia – her attributes becoming narrower as time passed. She was depicted as the Queen of Hell in the gnostic fourth-century text *Pistis Sophia* and invoked by Shakespeare in *Macbeth*'s 'dagger' soliloquy: 'Witchcraft celebrates pale Hecate's offerings ...'. Despite a more nuanced depiction in Blake's painting *The Night of Enitharmon's Joy*, she remained, until very recently, a one-dimensional wicked goddess of witchcraft.

However, Hecate's tattered reputation has latterly been somewhat stitched. Granted, some of that change has been due to the goddess' modishly gothic appearance, contemporary fashion designers seizing on this most glamorous of goddesses as a muse. Jean-Paul Gaultier named a feather-bedecked black coat dress after her, Mary Katrantzou based a collection on Greek goddesses and priestesses starring Hecate, while Alexander McQueen built a career on her glitteringly dark aesthetic.

Yet there is more to this goddess' comeback than catwalk gloss. Strip away the robes and glamour and you'll uncover her compassion. Her nocturnal life and preference for liminal spaces make her attractive to marginalised groups such as the homeless, sex workers, those in transient lifestyles, members of the LGBT+ community, people with mental illnesses and those who choose to worship in different ways.

More widely still, her unflinching attitude towards the biggest of life's transitions – birth and death – makes her a companion for both the most joyful and darkest of times. Mortality is the last great taboo in modern society but a subject that is now just beginning to be spoken about candidly, with the emergence of death-positive movements such as The Order of the Good Death. Hecate has been helping humans face their final journeys for centuries. It's reassuring to think that perhaps she is still there to hold women's hands and shine her torches through the dark as we go into labour, nurse children and face our final days.

MORGAN
LE FAY

**BRITISH: ENCHANTRESS
AND FAIRY**

Also known as
Morgen
Morgan(n)a
Morgain(e)
Morgane
Morgant(e)

The morally ambivalent, sexually knowing character of Morgan Le Fay has been portrayed over time as a healer, a necromancer, a scholar and a shape shifter. A lead character in the tales of King Arthur, she is, in turn, both the king's protector and his nemesis. It's this complexity and fluidity that has fascinated readers for hundreds of years.

Morgan's origins are as misty as the lake of Avalon. Did she morph from the triple goddess Morrígan? Is her name really a corruption of Modron, the wife of Urien and mother of Owein, in Welsh legend? Or was her character established in the early medieval sagas – a fairy queen who could travel on or under water?

She first steps into Arthur's mythos in Geoffrey of Monmouth's *Vita Merlini*, written in 1150. Here, she is the eldest of the nine sisters who rule the ethereal isle of Avalon and is a powerful healer. This Morgan could shape shift into animals, manifest as a crone or a maiden and fly, 'Like Daedalus, on strange wings'. She's also clever – a skilled mathematician and astronomer. Arthur's men trust Morgan and take their mortally injured king to her to be healed. Geoffrey's portrayal of her is sympathetic and he creates a strong, rounded female character.

In Chrétien de Troyes' French romantic interpretation of the myth, she is presented as Arthur's sister and described as 'Morgan the Wise'. She is no longer the ruler of the island, but is in a relationship with its ruler, Lord Guigomar. And so her power starts to be subsumed, manipulated by medieval writers, reluctant to believe a woman could be knowledgeable, powerful or clever.

She remains a relatively benign character until Arthur's tale is dramatically rewritten in the French *Vulgate Cycle* (c. 1210– 30), thought to be composed by fundamentalist Cistercian monks. Cistercians were crusaders, dedicated to eradicating heretics. They despised women – some even argued against the existence of a female soul – and used the Arthurian tales as propaganda for the Christian religion. Morgan embodied everything that terrified them about the old forms of worship – a knowledgeable, gifted woman, unashamed of her flesh and desires, existing in a society that acknowledged a female presence. They twisted the benevolent character of Morgan Le Fay into a more sinister seductress and obsessive witch.

Their Morgan is Arthur's older half-sister, aunt of the traitor Mordred. She is described as both beautiful and ugly – that duality again – a hard worker and a highly accomplished student of Merlin. However, she is also 'the most lustful woman in all Great Britain and the lewdest'. This lust is directed towards Queen Guinevere's nephew, Guiomar. On discovering the affair, and perhaps jealous of Morgan's kinship with Arthur, the Queen separates the lovers, leading Morgan's obsessive, vengeful side to be unleashed.

Using her looks and sexuality, she persuades Merlin to teach her the dark arts. She exposes Guinevere's affair with Lancelot and later tries to seduce the knight. In the order's later works, Morgan's character becomes more overtly evil: she uses her powers to steal the magical sword Excalibur and its scabbard to use against Arthur and plots his downfall, only to be thwarted by the new witch Ninianne, the Lady of the Lake. However, at the end of *Vulgate Cycle*, Morgan is one of the ladies who escort Arthur on his final trip to Avalon. By 1485, when the definitive

Arthur book, *Le Morte d'Arthur* by Thomas Malory, appears, the Cistercian template is set. Malory's Morgan is even more reductive. There is no affair that initiates her conflict with Guinevere; instead she's just a fundamentally wicked person, malevolent, Arthur's nemesis, a mistress of the dark arts, manifesting the medieval world's fear of the knowledge and power of women.

In Germany, the *Malleus Maleficarum* (Hammer of Witches) was about to be published near-simultaneously and these books helped to whip up anti-magic fervour and presaged a spike in UK witch trials. One last vestige of Morgan's earlier incarnation remains – she is permitted to transport Arthur's body to Avalon.

Morgan has remained a powerful figure in literature – she appears in Italian Renaissance poems, French literature and English writer Edmund Spenser's epic poem *The Faerie Queen*. She has smouldered on the big screen, memorably portrayed by Helen Mirren in *Excalibur* (1981). More recently, she has been a villain in Marvel and DC comic books.

'Men believe beyond proof to the contrary that blood is thicker than water and that a beautiful woman cannot be evil.'
– JOHN STEINBECK, *THE ACTS OF KING ARTHUR AND HIS NOBLE KNIGHTS*

Her character is strong enough to bear endless reworking. The image of a sexually confident woman, clever, and gifted with magical healing abilities has been reimagined from benevolent to evil, yet still retains its power. Scared authors turned Morgan into an evil, vengeful caricature – the only way they could deal with her independence, her power, her sexuality.

All her incarnations have something to offer and hearten; the wise healer of the early depictions with her grasp of the powers of the divine feminine is a blue-chip inspiration, of course. Yet the later, reworked, sinister Morgan has merit too – political knowledge, clever strategic thinking and academic prowess. Her control and confidence in her own seductive power are incredibly important. Even her vengeful, destructive tendencies serve as a reminder that everyone has a malevolent side; her rage is wild and to be feared and respected. If anything, the contradictions in Morgan's character are what make her intriguing and relatable. From mothering, healing goddess to wrathful, powerful enemy, Morgan Le Fay embodies all our most secret, darkest and sweetest ambitions.

CIRCE

Also known as
Κίρκη
Kirke
Pure Mother Bee

With her wand, spells, herbs and transfigurative powers, Circe was the first witch of Western literature; she set a template for enchantresses down the centuries. However, this lone wolf goddess had a very human core.

Born into a family of powerful sorceresses on the fringes of the Greek mythos, Circe was the daughter of Perse, an Oceanid nymph, and Helios, a Titan who represented the sun. Her sister, Pasiphae, was a witch who possessed a nerdy knowledge of herbal magic; she was the mother of the Minotaur. Her brothers were Aeetes, who guarded the Golden Fleece, and Perses, who was murdered by Medea, a deeply powerful witch. Confusingly, Medea was Circe's niece, as well as the wife of Jason (of the Argonauts fame). Your standard dysfunctional family of deities, then.

Circe lived what appears to be an idyllic, solitary life on the island of Aiaia. According to some, she had been banished there by her father after murdering her husband, a Prince of Colchis, but other storytellers infer that she lived in luxurious solitary confinement

out of choice. She spent her time honing her enviable magic spells, collecting herbs from the thick forest that fringed her land and doting on her magically docile pet lions and wolves. There was the occasional visitor however. As Ovid tells it, Glaucus, a sea god, once called by to ask her advice on love. He'd fallen for a nymph, Scylla, who wasn't keen on his half-fish appearance. Circe, however, wanted Glaucus for herself, so she poured a potion into Scylla's bathing water, transforming the beautiful nymph into a monster with six dog heads, twelve tentacles and a cat's tail.

PIGGING OUT

Circe is perhaps most famous for the role she plays in Homer's *Odyssey*. According to the book, when they landed on Aiaia, Odysseus' men were exhausted after ten years at sea. In their most recent battle with man-eating giants the Laestrygonians, they had lost eleven of their twelve ships. Odysseus sent out an advance search party of the remaining crew who found Circe's mansion.

In some readings, the goddess is scheming and wicked; she entertains the men hospitably, flirting, feeding them, singing and encouraging them to forget their wives and homes, then, in a flash, turns on them, waves her wand and transforms them into pigs. However, a more realistic reading might be that she is aware of being outnumbered and vulnerable, so makes a wary, pre-emptive strike – perhaps her knowledge of herbs allowed her to add a hallucinogenic to their food, conjuring up their beastly transformation. That she turns the crew into swine, foreshadowing the second-wave feminist cry of 'male chauvinist pigs', just adds to the resonance of her actions.

Odysseus, wondering what has happened to his men, follows their trail. On his way inland, he meets the messenger god Hermes, who tells him to use a herb, moly, to shield himself from Circe's enchantments. He also tells Odysseus that to dominate Circe, he must sleep with her. Odysseus heads to Circe's mansion and drinks the potion she offers, which, of course, has no effect. He holds his sword against her throat. It's probably important to remember who Ovid's narrator is at this point – Odysseus. He maintains that Circe submits willingly, in a heavily euphemistic speech: 'Put up your weapon in the sheath. We two shall mingle and make love upon our bed. So mutual trust may come of play and love.'

In similarly immodest fashion, Odysseus tells how, after they've shared a bed, Circe immediately falls in love with him, releasing his men from their enchantment. They all stay on the island for a year – according to Ovid, blissfully. Hesiod's version of the story even tells how Circe bears Odysseus three sons in this time – but after twelve months his men persuade him to go home. Perhaps here, we get a glimpse of Circe's real feelings for Odysseus – she literally tells him to go to hell, warning: 'You must go to the house of Hades and of dread Proserpine to consult the ghost of the blind Theban prophet Teiresias.' Did she resent Odysseus' leaving? Or was his year on the island forced upon her? Alternatively, was she really, as many retellings would have it, a cruel temptress who trapped Odysseus and his men on her island against their will?

The sexual and gender political tension on Circe's island has gripped writers for centuries, with Socrates, Ovid and James Joyce all retooling her story. There are Circe sculptures scattered around the world and her portrait hangs, with subtle differences, in a thousand galleries, while ballets explore her tale. Down the centuries, she has been used as a scapegoat: the men were turned into pigs thanks to her sexual desires or because she was a misandrist. She has been portrayed as temptress, witch, manhater. She personified the stereotype of women with power and knowledge as man-hungry and scheming.

'Odysseus, son of Laertes, the great traveller, prince of wiles and tricks and a thousand ways. He showed me his scars, and in return, he let me pretend that I had none.'
-MADELEINE MILLER, *CIRCE*

However, over the centuries, Circe's narrative has been reclaimed from cartoon witch to someone with more dimension. In 1999, Carol Ann Duffy gave voice to Circe in a wickedly funny poem recounting a recipe for pork, while Madeleine Miller's *Circe*, which topped the 2018 bestseller lists, details the intricate story of a woman who has to work at her craft and deal with the very mortal sides of being a mother.

Despite existing in a different civilisation, Circe's circumstances reflect that of many women today. She lives alone, indulging herself with her (big) cats and teaching herself new skills; independence personified. However, when people choose to walk into her world – and, as her home is an island, it is very much their choice – she will defend herself and stand her ground. She is a strategist with many tools: her deep voice commands; her magic protects.

Despite her immortality and enchantments, Circe is mortal. Although she is described as a goddess by some, her powers are self-taught: she has to work at them and practise like a human. Flesh figures more literally in her story too: she uses her body as a negotiating tool, she transforms men from human to beast and becomes a mother. She's an earthly witch, fallible, but happiest on her own with her pets and her herbs. No demands, no obligations, no having to fulfil society's requirements. She is, perhaps, just a woman who needs, in Virginia Woolf's famous words, 'a room of one's own'.

BABA YAGA

SLAVIC: WITCH

Also known as
Baba Jaga
Бába Ягá

The halfway point between Mother Earth and a cannabalistic crone, Baba Yaga is a mercurial character. Will she take you on a voyage of self-discovery and equip you with practical skills? Or throw you in her oven and gobble you up for tea?

You'll hear Baba Yaga before you spot her, a wild wind's whoosh, strong enough to make the trees creak and groan and tossing leaves into the air.

She is a fearful sight. Wisps of her long grey hair stream in the wind, her face dominated by a huge, pointy nose. Her skin is as deeply cracked as the steppe in summer, her mouth crammed with rusting iron teeth. She dresses in rags, is hunchbacked and flies around in an over-sized mortar, using a huge pestle to steer, while brushing away her trail with a reed-thin birch broom. Her home is no less attention-grabbing: behind a high wall made of bones and crenellated with fire-filled skulls lies a slope-roofed house on chicken legs that enable it to run wonkily through the woods. The hut can spin, it screeches and moans, it has eye-like windows and its lock is dense with teeth. At first glance, Baba Yaga appears to conform to the fairy-tale witch archetype. She can smell humans, has a predilection for the tender flesh of children and wields magic power. She commands three horsemen who represent 'bright dawn, red sun and dark midnight', and servants who are disembodied hands. However, the witch is a little more complex than she first appears. Visitors to her house may find themselves thrown onto a giant paddle and roasted in her oven, but they may also find that, in her own twisted, tortuous fashion, Baba Yaga can help them.

TALK TO THE HAND

Take the best-known tale starring Baba Yaga, 'Vasilisa the Beautiful', a folk story first anthologised by Russian Alexander Afanasyev in 1855. Here we find Vasilisa, losing her mother at a young age, and all she has left of her is a little magic doll who vows to protect the girl. In the way of these stories, into her life comes an evil stepmother and stepsisters who are jealous of Vasilisa's good looks. They all live in a little hut on the edge of a forbidding forest. One day, their fire sputters out, so they send Vasilisa into the trees to bring back one of Baba Yaga's flaming skulls. She arrives at the fowl-mounted hut where Baba Yaga hisses at her, 'Listen girl! If I give you a light you must work to pay for it. If not, I will eat you for my supper!'

Over two days, she sets the girl a series of repetitive, boring domestic tasks, which, to the crone's surprise – and with a little help from her magic doll – she completes. When the tasks are finished, Vasilisa asks Baba Yaga who each of the witch's horsemen are. Baba Yaga answers gladly. Vasilisa is itching to ask about the hand-shaped servants, but has a feeling that might be a terrible idea, so stays silent. Baba Yaga informs her that her intuition was right – that had she enquired about them, Vasilisa would have ended up on the paddle being pushed into the oven.

'Naughty children have to be protected. Even if it's just from themselves.'
– MARIKA McCOOLA, *BABA YAGA'S ASSISTANT*

Then Baba asks the girl a question, 'How is it that you have been able to finish all the work I gave you so quickly?' The girl replies, 'My mother's blessing helped me!' At this, Baba Yaga flies into a spitting rage and pushes her out of the hut. However, simultaneously she thrusts one of her flaming skulls onto a stick and pushes it into Vasilisa's hands. The girl eventually finds her way home and gives the skull to her scheming family. Her mother and sisters burst into flames and dissolve into ashes. Vasilisa is free.

This story illustrates Baba Yaga's duality and subverts the fairy-tale archetype. Baba Yaga helps Vasilisa, but in a roundabout way. Yaga rewards Vasilisa for listening to her intuition as represented by the doll. It's not a convenient, neat result for the girl though: she has to find her own path. Author Clarissa Pinkola Estes argues that, in doing this, Vasilisa is initiated into finding her own 'wild feminine power'. The hut serves almost as a women's retreat, where she finds her core through 'inner purifications' – or 'grindingly dull tasks' as they are otherwise known – and by asking questions about the horsemen, or rather puzzling over the nature of life and death.

Baba Yaga often reaches out to young women on the cusp of adulthood whom she deems worthy of her attention, steering them into the next stage of life. In the tales gathered in Sibelan Forrester's 2013 *Baba Yaga: The Wild Witch of the East in Russian Fairy Tales*, she repeatedly challenges girls to step up to the duties needed for them to become wives and mothers – important lessons in a society that values those traits highly.

Baba Yaga is thought to have haunted the folk tales of Russia and beyond for centuries, but she was first referred to in print in 1855, in Mikhail V. Lomonosov's *Rossiiskaia Grammatika*. One of the composer Mussorgsky's pieces from *Pictures at an Exhibition*, 'The Hut on Hen's Legs', references her and she has been the subject of many films, including the seminal fantasy movie *Vasilissa The Beautiful* (1939). She also inspired the Yubaba character in *Spirited Away* (2001).

Baba Yaga's feral qualities and liminal status are also her powers. She doesn't conform to accepted norms; her hair is unbraided and stands on end, her fingernails long, her breasts drooping and unfettered. She dresses in tatters, while her unconventional accommodation arrangements are almost like a piece of outsider art. She lives not only on the fringes of habitation, but also outside of society's mores. Baba Yaga exists how she chooses and has no need for others in her life, bar her hand-shaped servants and horsemen. She refuses to conform, even to conventional evil witch stereotypes. A wild woman yet wise teacher, she lives life unbound, only giving an inch to those she deems worthy of her knowledge. Who could fail to admire such a gleefully wild spirit?

CASSANDRA

GREEK: PROPHET

Gifted and cursed with the power of accurate prophecy, Cassandra's name is now given to those who tell the truth, yet are vilified. Her determination and refusal to be silenced continue to inspire campaigners and those pushing for justice thousands of years down the line.

Cassandra was the radiant and clever daughter of Troy's King Priam and Queen Hecuba. One story tells how the god Apollo granted her the supernatural gift of being able to predict events in childhood, but in another, it was bestowed by him in Cassandra's teenage years – in return, he hoped, for sexual favours. In both traditions, Cassandra refused him that pleasure: her body, her decision. However, her unwavering courage did not go unpunished.

Apollo was furious and briefly considered raping Cassandra. However, he knew how angry this would make his sister, Athena, who was Cassandra's protector. Instead, the god inverted the abilities he had given the girl: he spat into her mouth and from that moment her gift became a curse, the prophecies

remaining accurate, but no one believing them. They were, as the epic poet Quintus Smyrnaeus said, 'as idle wind in the hearers' ears'.

We can only imagine the frustration of Cassandra; her visions were clear and yet when she tried to warn her family and the Trojan people of disasters on the horizon, she was dismissed as a mad woman. However, she would not be silenced, bravely continuing to speak out even when she was dismissed by her friends, family and neighbours. She told the truth even when it brought her pain and humiliation.

She taught her brother Helenus the art of prediction, but in an ancient twist on the hepeating paradox (where a woman is ignored only to have a man save the day by repeating what she's already said), her male sibling's prophecies were believed. Helenus and Cassandra both prophesised that, should the beautiful Queen Helen ever enter the city, then Troy would fall. So when their brother Paris brought Helen back to the city as his dazzling new wife, Cassandra physically attacked 'the face that launched a thousand ships' in a vain attempt to prevent her from entering the gates. Helen's ex-husband, King Menelaus, was hot on his wandering wife's heels and, as Cassandra had predicted, went to war against the Trojans. So started a siege of the city that would last nearly ten years.

A GIFT OR CURSE?

Cassandra's most famous prophecy related to the giant wooden horse wheeled into Troy as a 'gift' from the Greeks who, after nearly a decade, were desperate to breach the walls of the city. Rocked by the forceful image of soldiers hiding inside the timber steed, she warned the people of Troy of the danger. They merely laughed and, according to Quintus Smyrnaeus, taunted her, saying, 'No maiden modesty with purity veils thee: thou art compassed round with ruinous madness; therefore all men scorn thee, babbler!' In desperation, Cassandra grabbed a blazing branch and double-edged spear and ran bravely towards the wheeled stallion, determined to destroy it. However, she was captured, her weapons taken away and she was escorted from the scene.

That night, the hidden army emerged from the belly of the beast and opened the gates of the city to their comrades. Fleeing the rampage, Cassandra hid in one of Athena's temples, but was followed by the aptly named Ajax the Lesser who raped her so brutally that Athena's statue cried copious tears. Cassandra was brought as a trophy to Agamemnon, King of Mycenae, who took her as a slave and a concubine.

Despite her horrendous experiences, Cassandra remained unbowed; she knew that eventually her enforced relationship with Agamemnon would result in both his death and her own – a revenge of sorts. According to Euripides' *The Trojan Women and Hippolytus*, she murmured, chin out, 'the famed king of the Achaeans will find me a bride more difficult to manage than Helen'. As ever, her prediction was correct. Some years later, Cassandra, Agamemnon and their children were murdered by the king's wife, Clytemnestra, and her lover, Aegisthus.

Cassandra has remained a popular cultural touchstone down the millennia, appearing in poems, plays – notably William Shakespeare's *Troilus and Cressida* – and in Florence Nightingale's unpublished essay named after the prophet, in which she protests against the restrictions placed on upper-class English women in the mid-1800s. In the early 1980s, Cassandra became canonised as a feminist icon by Christa Wolf in her novel *Cassandra*, which gave a voice to the prophet – telling the Trojan narrative from her point of view and serving as an allegory for the author's own life under the oppressive East German political regime.

'I prefer to see myself as the Janus, the two-faced god who is half Pollyanna, half Cassandra, warning of the future and perhaps living too much in the past.'
– RAY BRADBURY

So universal, in fact, is the story of Cassandra's curse, that it lends its name to a syndrome – the Cassandra complex, where truthful warnings are dismissed, notably in the fields of environmental action and equality. Those who warn about climate change have traditionally been ridiculed as hippies or fearmongers, even as it becomes increasingly clear that there's a vital point to be made. Similarly, Cassandra's experiences echo those of modern assault victims; they are often disbelieved, doubted and discounted. As recently as 2017, it took thousands of women to form a critical mass before the #MeToo movement against sexual harassment and violence started to gain traction.

Cassandra lived at a time when women were expected to be reserved, silent, and to smilingly allow men the stage. Her story demonstrates how those who tried to speak out, who wanted to be heard, were condemned as insane. But still she refuses to be quieted. She doesn't hide her talent and continues to warn her people of impending danger. When it's clear others don't believe her, she even tries to take action herself. She is salty, brave, owns her 'mad' image and is determined not to be shut down. She is stoic – even her final words in Aeschylus' *Agamemnon* drip with empathy for her oppressors, 'I'm just a killed slave, easy fistful of death. But you, O humans, O human things – when a man is happy, a shadow could overturn it … You, you, I pity.'

THE PYTHIA

A priestess with a hotline to the divine, the Pythia's womanly wisdom was held sacred by politicians, warriors and strategists, and gave a loud, clear voice to women in Greek society.

A woman sits, knees drawn up, in a cauldron suspended on a tall, golden tripod. In one hand, she holds a bunch of laurel leaves, in the other, a dish of spring water; she is clothed in a short, white dress. Below her, a crack in the ground belches out thick vapours. Engulfed in the sweet fumes, her eyes roll back into her head, her hair becomes wild; she starts to foam at the mouth and sway from side to side, arms in the air. In this heightened state, she begins to tell the future. This is the Pythia.

The Pythia was not a singular person, but a title passed from woman to woman. The name was given to the high priestess picked to become the oracle at the Temple of Apollo, in Delphi, Greece. From the end of the seventh century BCE to the fourth century CE, this series of women delivered prophecies directly from Apollo, god of healing, light and prophecy.

The imposing temple of Delphi sits high on the western slope of Mount Parnassus. Some believe that the place was originally the site of a female-led Gaia-worshipping cult, while later, others held it to be the centre of the earth. Another story tells how Apollo killed Python, son of Gaia and guardian of the temple, and threw his body into the crevasse, thus claiming the place for himself. As the body rotted, it emitted the intoxicating gases that swirled around the altar. A more prosaic take was that the original female-run temple was annexed by priests from Delos in the eighth century BCE and the incomers kept the tradition of priestesses running the oracle to placate locals. Whichever story is closest to the truth, this site was hugely important to Greeks – and the establishment of the Apollo-centred temple was celebrated with four-yearly games.

HONOUR OR SACRIFICE?

The Pythia was initially chosen from highly educated, morally 'pure' young virgins, but after the military officer Echecrates the Thessalian raped one of the women post-consultation in the third century BCE, the priestess was replaced by an older woman, dressed in virginal robes. Later, the education and social standing of the prophet became less important, with peasants being just as likely to take to the cauldron.

The chosen woman was expected to make sacrifices. And not just of goats. She was required to give up her family, her home and her individuality; she became the Pythia, consumed by the role. The job was physically and mentally demanding, the career – and life – of the prophet was short. Perhaps because of these demands, the timetabling of the prophecies was limited. Once a month during the summer, although at the height of the Oracle's popularity, there were three Pythia at one time manning the prophecy bucket.

Before each session, the priestess would undergo purification rituals, bathing in the Castalian Spring, fasting and drinking the waters of the Cassotis Spring. The ceremony would be prefaced with the killing of a goat and payment from the questioner. However, rather than direct visions of the future, the priestess most often dispensed sage advice. The Pythia's proclamations were sometimes obtuse – such as the bet-hedging reply to a man asking if he should join the army: 'Go, return not die in war.' At other times, they were precise, colourful, unambiguous stanzas.

When the Athenians consulted the oracle, fearful of an attack from Xerxes, their fears were confirmed. They were told: 'Now your statues are standing and pouring sweat. They shiver with dread. The black blood drips from the highest rooftops. They have seen the necessity of evil. Get out, get out of my sanctum and drown your spirits in woe.'

Rather tragically, the Pythia was so self-aware, she even foretold her own redundancy. In the mid-fourth century CE, Julian the Apostate, a Roman emperor, attempted a revival of classical Greek culture and consulted the oracle. The Pythia mournfully said: 'Tell to the king that the cavern wall is fallen in decay; Apollo has no chapel left, no prophesying bay, No talking stream. The stream is dry that had so much to say.'

There is plenty of historical evidence for the existence of the Pythia. In the 1980s, geological investigation revealed that the site sat on the intersection of two major fissures, which would have resulted in high levels of ethylene, a gas known to induce hallucinogenic states, leaking through. As described by Plutarch, a writer and first-century priest at Delphi, the effects displayed by the Pythia were remarkably similar. He ascribed the powers partly to the fumes, but mainly to the woman's training and preparation. Rather beautifully, he said that Apollo was the musician, the Pythia a lyre and the gas emissions the musical ability.

Although the Pythia are not mythological, they sit in the murky, halfway house that encompasses witches and those with supernatural powers, communing with gods. Those powers were not insignificant; the fate of not just individuals, but armies and nations might lie in the hands of those manning the Oracle. Reading the prophecies now, they often advocate peaceful, wise solutions – what could be seen as a female perspective. Despite the somewhat weak narrative of the Pythia as the mortal mouthpiece of Apollo, the Delphic Oracle may have allowed Greek leaders to take on board the valuable opinions of women without being seen to be emasculated. The Oracle gave Greek women a powerful voice: the priestesses were highly regarded in society, rewarded with tax breaks and luxurious apartments.

> 'We should hear the cause that has made the Pythia cease to prophesy ... either the Pythia does not get near the spot where the Divinity is ... or the power has failed.'
> – PLUTARCH

The Pythia are, perhaps, the epitome of the spiritual woman, with a hotline to the divine. Their costume, preparation and ecstatic trances still find their place in today's world, and not just in the formalised ceremonies and women's circles of neopaganists or on suburban stages hosting quack mystic acts. Who hasn't got a friend who regularly pulls on her best frock, goes out dancing, then, at the after party, dispenses, what seems at the time, the most wise advice? But, of course, the Pythia represent much more than that. These were women who had a career – one in which they were listened to on a national and international level and had given up their private lives in order to pursue that work – and whose voices were valued and acted upon. These women were regarded as important.

We may think that we are living in the age of progress and equality, but perhaps would-be politicians, diplomats and heads of state could learn something from the esteem in which these wise women were held.

BERCHTA

**SOUTHERN GERMAN/
AUSTRIAN: GODDESS**

Also known as
Perchta
Bertha
Percht

This wild, frosty goddess is harsh on those she deems to have broken her domestic rules, but crack Berchta's icy exterior and you'll find a warm, tender heart.

Berchta is having something of a fashion moment. Alongside her male counterpart, Krampus, she dominates Alpine winter social media feeds. Both mythological figures have their own parades which take place in towns in the snowy mountains. Krampus has his runs, Instagram-friendly, pre-Christmas festivals where people in wooden, beast-like masks with horns and hairy costumes strewn with bells throw fireworks about, making as much noise as possible. Berchta follows hard on her cousin's heels with her *Perchtenlauf* processions, which take place in the period leading up to Epiphany in early January. These parties bring together another baying collection of terrifyingly costumed people aiming to scare away the cold winter spirits and the icy weather they bring.

There's much more to this goddess than joke-shop masks and Glühwein-fuelled mayhem, however: she's played many characters in her surprisingly long life.

The medieval Berchta was demanding of German women, deeming that they should not weave on the Epiphany, her special day. Her role subtly changed as women's labour became more essential: she required them not just to keep a tidy house, but also to spin all their allotted flax on time – and to leave a bowl of porridge for her on her festival night. In return, she might leave rewards such as wood chips that turned to gold for the hardest workers. The punishment for transgressing these rules was harsh. Berchta might tear you from your bed, rip open your belly, pull out your guts, stuff the cavity with straw and rocks and then stitch your stomach up, leaving you as a half-human, half-scarecrow hybrid.

Despite her violent behaviour, Berchta often manifested as a beautiful snow queen, ethereal and icy, pale-faced with a whisper of blush and frosted eyelashes. More scarily, she sometimes appeared as an old hag, sporting a hooked, iron nose and messy hair, one large bird foot protruding from under her long, dirty skirts – a distant cousin, perhaps, of Baba Yaga (see pages 22–25). Sometimes, she was a mix of the two, maiden and crone, thought by some to be an echo of the double-faced Finnish Loviator (see pages 110–13). This duality is represented in some of today's festivals held in her name, where you'll find both beautiful and ugly versions of Berchta.

'People who have not been in Narnia sometimes think that a thing cannot be good and terrible at the same time.'

– C.S.LEWIS, *THE LION, THE WITCH AND THE WARDROBE*

Folk tale collector Jacob Grimm was fascinated by this wild, forest-dwelling creature. He believed she had been around since at least the tenth century and was determined to strip away the witch caricature that he believed had been imposed by the Church to discover the more layered character beneath.

Grimm's nineteenth-century *Teutonic Mythology* tells how Berchta and her coterie would be abroad in the period between Christmas and Twelfth Night, the Rauhnächte, 'when the supernatural has sway'. He describes her at the head of the Wild Hunt, a furious ride, peopled with the 'berchten' – demons, spirits, witches and the souls of unbaptised children, who galloped across the skies on horseback, waging war with other gods or bringing abundance to the earth. The parades that still take place today have echoes of the hunt – a retinue of beasts rampaging, with much noise and chaos. Grimm believed another German goddess, Holda, was a parallel incarnation of Berchta. She lived in the north of the country and was the patron of farming and crafts. Grimm traced a line between these women and Odin's wife, Frigg, or her doppelgänger Freyja (see pages 60–63), who also used to thunder across the night sky.

Grimm dug deep to find the softer side of Berchta, emphasising her patronage of spinners, which places her firmly into the pan-European group of goddesses whose weaving was wefted to the fate of man. It's no surprise that she absorbs so many characteristics of deities from across Europe – Germany is right at the heart of the landmass. Reading between the lines of Grimm's descriptions of these fierce, north European goddesses, you'll catch tantalising glimpses of their pre-Christian origins as 'psychopomps', spirits who accompany souls to the afterlife.

Berchta and her associated goddesses were particularly associated with the spirits of dead children. Grimm tells a story of a grieving mother who met her daughter's soul as it accompanied Berchta on her Rauhnächte hunts. The girl told her to stop crying, that her tears had already filled a jug that was too heavy to carry. These stories served a purpose, to reassure grief-stricken mothers in a time of high infant mortality.

Children across the country also knew Berchta and Holda for a more positive reason; they were credited with creating the first snows of winter as they shook out their goose-feather beds, the birds' white down escaping across the leaden skies. There were more connections to the long-necked bird; Holda wears a goose-down cape and in illustrations Berchta is often depicted accompanied by geese, and she has her water bird's foot. Some believe her to be the root of the Mother Goose tale. So, somewhere in history, she developed a dual personality – one aspect of her cuddly, neutered persona even becoming embedded in fairy tales, the other blackened as Christianity took hold of the country.

Berchta's story was rewritten by the Christian Church. She was portrayed as evil, more crone-like and reduced to little more than a caricature of a witch. Why? Because she represented pagan elements that the Church wanted suppressed and demonisation was the easiest way to ruin her reputation and kill her worship. The custom of leaving food out for her and her followers in exchange for wealth and bountiful harvests was explicitly condemned in Bavaria, southern Germany, in the fifteenth-century texts *Thesaurus pauperum* and *De decem praeceptis*. However, so vivid was the character of this pagan goddess that she lived on in folk memory, in customs, place names such as Berchtesgaden in the Bavarian Alps, in festivals and in the local name of the night of the Epiphany, Berchtentag.

Although tourists now flock to join the demonic parades held in Berchta's name and know her as an evil entity, perhaps it's time to look beyond the animal masks and horns, the bogeywoman tales of stomach-ripping and punishments and see the genuine goodness beneath. There is something wildly romantic, touching even, about the original Snow Queen Berchta in her serene beauty and deep love of children. It's as if Narnia's White Witch grew a heart, that her offer of Turkish delight was real and that there really is a place in her palace for all the lost girls and boys.

WHITE
BUFFALO CALF
WOMAN

**INDIGENOUS AMERICAN/
LAKOTAN: SPIRIT**

Also known as
Pte San Win
Ptesan Winyan
Ptehincala San Win

Loving the earth and smoking pipes, the
White Buffalo Calf Woman was the original
hippy. She taught the Lakota Sioux tribes their
most precious ceremonies, as well as vital
environmental lessons. But this eco-warrior and
educator wasn't all love and peace.

Nineteen generations, or 2,000 years ago, the tribes
of the Lakota Sioux people in North America came
together for the seven sacred council fires. The
gathering was marred by a lack of food – there were
no animals to be found. So, one morning, the chief
of the Itazipcho tribe sent two young men out to
hunt. After a long and fruitless search, they decided

to climb a hill in order to survey the land. As they ascended, they saw a figure floating towards them, a woman dressed in white buckskin, embroidered with colourful designs. She had long black hair, worn loose but for a bunch tied up with buffalo fur. Her eyes shone with knowledge and she radiated holiness.

The first scout was filled with uncontrollable lust for this incredible woman. He said to his friend, 'We can do what we want to and no one will ever know.' 'Hang on,' said the other man. 'Doesn't this woman deserves our respect?' The first hunter laughed and ran towards the girl, his sinister intentions clear. As he reached her and embraced this vision in white, a cloud engulfed the pair and lightning bolts flashed. As the cloud settled, the second scout was horrified to see the woman standing calmly next to a pile of blackened bones – all that remained of his friend. Terrified, he drew his bow. However, the woman spoke calmly to him in his own language: 'Don't be scared. Return to the camp and tell them I'm coming. Ask them to prepare for my arrival.'

The man sprinted back to camp and the tribes erected their biggest tipi ready for the mysterious visitor. Four days later, as promised, she arrived. Over the next four days, the woman showed them how to make a sacred altar of red earth, then drew from her backpack a *chanunpa*, or sacred pipe. She taught them how to fill the pipe with *chan-shasha*, a tobacco made from red willow bark, to sing the pipe-filling song and then she whispered instructions for the Lakota's seven sacred ceremonies. She showed them how to care for the land, revealing to them that all things in the world are connected and asking them always to bear in mind that children are the future. These are the building blocks still at the foundation of today's environmental movement.

She promised to return when she was needed, in the form of a white animal. As she walked away into the sunset, she suddenly stopped, rolling over to emerge in the form of a black buffalo. Again she tumbled down, but this time she turned into a brown buffalo. On her third somersault, she became a red beast. On her fourth and final spin, she turned into the most sacred of all beasts, a white buffalo calf, before disappearing.

As soon as she vanished, herds of buffalo roared over the hill crest. Buffalo are the bedrock of Native American culture, providing food, skins for clothes and shelter and bones for tools, and are seen as symbols of abundance and sacred life. The woman who brought these vital sources of life to the people was given the name Pte San Win or White Buffalo Calf

Woman. Some believe that the Dakota goddess of harmony and peace, Wóȟpe, who fell to earth like a meteorite, was another manifestation.

Although women are usually seen as subservient to men in Native American culture – one of the Sioux's mottos is 'woman shall not walk before man' – this goddess, the people's most important supernatural entity, is female. She serves to teach the Lakota tribes not only how to smoke the sacred pipe, but how to live together in harmony as human beings. That said, she wasn't all about love – she knocked back that lustful hunter in spectacularly violent fashion.

THE GREAT DEFENDER

Her elevation of women is honoured by members of the Lakota tribe who established a society, White Buffalo Calf Women's Society (WBCWS), in the 1970s, offering shelter to victims of domestic violence, sexual assault and stalking. As a proverb from the nearby Cheyenne tribe has it: 'As long as the hearts of our women are high, the nation will live. But should the hearts of our women be on the ground, then all is lost.' Her sacred bundle and pipe remain on earth, guarded by generations of Native Americans; their keeper now is environmental activist Arvol Looking Horse.

The births in the 1990s and early 2000s of white buffalo calves were seen by the indigenous American people to be worrying portents. Eco-aware followers of White Buffalo Calf Woman feel as if they are living through the prophecy that the animals would appear again at a time of strife; they see climate change as that dire emergency. The White Buffalo Calf Woman is being called upon again to help protect the country and world she loves. Will she rise once more to the occasion?

RHIANNON

CELTIC: GODDESS/FAIRY

She may appear to be a bohemian dreamer, but this goddess' gentle, magical appearance belies a steely core. This animal-loving fairy princess has grit and determination in abundance.

Goddess of the moon, Rhiannon is a beautiful maiden, often found to be riding her beloved white horse or even manifesting in equine form. Behind her fly her three magical birds, said to sing songs that can heal all sadness, wake the dead from their slumber and send the living whistling happily to their doom. Rhiannon first appears in the *Mabinogion*, the twelfth- to thirteenth-century collection of stories that are believed to be the earliest British prose literature. These tales are gathered in four branches and bring together oral pre-Christian Celtic mythology and folklore stories in written form, including those of King Arthur.

Rhiannon was the daughter of Hefaidd Hen, the Lord of the Otherworld. Her father had promised her hand in marriage to Gwawl ap Clud, a minor sun god, but Rhiannon thought he was repugnant. A union with Hefaidd Hen's daughter would have been a powerful

'She's bold, strong, and
forthright. She spots her man,
then gets him. Twice over.'

political move; many human families legitimised themselves
by claiming faerie ancestry (see The Lady of Llyn y Fan Fach,
pages 157–59).

DREAMY BUT DETERMINED

According to one tale, one day, Rhiannon was out riding,
dressed in her finest gold silks and moving in her trademark
dreamy, slow fashion. She was spotted by the Prince of Dyfed,
Pwyll, who instantly fell in love with her and sent his fastest
horseman to give chase. However, he could not keep up with
Rhiannon. The next day, Pwyll returned. Again he sent his
horseman after her and again he failed to catch up with her.
On the third day, Pwyll gave chase himself and on this occasion
managed to keep pace with the princess. Finally, he asked her to
stop. Rhiannon rebuked him for taking his time, saying, wryly:
'Of course I'll stop, and it would have been better for your horse
if you had asked me before.' Consequently, it became obvious
that Rhiannon had sought out Pwyll for herself.

The pair decided to marry and, on the appointed day, all
seemed well. The feast was prepared and Pwyll was welcomed
into Rhiannon's father's palace. However, as they sat down to
eat, a mysterious visitor appeared and asked a favour of Pwyll.
Happy and slightly drunk, the prince agreed, upon which the
stranger revealed himself as Gwawl. Rhiannon was furious with
Pwyll, calling him a fool. ('Never did man make worse use of his
wits than thou hast done.') She had prepared a cunning plan,
however: 'Pretend to give me to him – I promise that I'll never
really be his.'

A year passed and this time Rhiannon and Gwawl's wedding
day dawned. However, Rhiannon had tipped off Pwyll and he
waited outside with a hundred of his men. At the height of
the celebrations, Pwyll entered, disguised as a tramp with an
enchanted leather bag that Rhiannon had given him slung over
his shoulder. Pwyll asked Gwawl to fill the bag with food. The sun

god tried to fill it, but to no avail, so peeked inside. Immediately, Pwyll fastened it over Gwawl's head, encouraging his men to beat him with sticks until he submitted. The vanquishing of the sun god Gwawl is said to represent the festival of Samhain, or the end of summer.

Pwyll became Rhiannon's husband, but it was not happy ever after. Rhiannon had trouble conceiving, eventually giving birth to a son. On the night he was born, the women watching over him fell asleep and the boy vanished. The guilty women smeared Rhiannon with puppy blood, before swearing that she had eaten her own child. As a punishment, the princess was made to sit outside the palace on a block, telling every guest of her horrendous deeds and offering to carry them on her back into the palace, like a horse. Most guests refused as she was so humble and beautiful. After two years, a couple who found the boy (who had grown at a supernatural pace) realised his identity and returned him to an overjoyed Rhiannon. He was renamed Pryderi and, on his father's death, became King of Dyfed. Pryderi and Rhiannon went on to have more adventures documented in the *Mabinogion*. She later married her son's friend, Manawydan, and they travelled England.

It's believed that Rhiannon's story may have its roots in a primitive Celtic female deity and she has also been linked to the Gallo-Roman horse goddess Epona. In recent years, the Wiccan movement has portrayed her as a rather one-dimensional benevolent, smiling figure. However, the Rhiannon who appears in the *Mabinogion* has more grit than that of the winsome image on New Age tarots, the crystal shop pin-up or the floaty hippy portrayed in the Fleetwood Mac song that takes her name. She has gumption, determines her fate, shapes her own future. She chooses who she wants to marry, then carries out not one, but two cunning plans to ensure that it happens. She's bold, strong, and forthright. She spots her man, then gets him. Twice over.

She is also stoic: despite knowing that she is innocent of murder, she serves out her punishment with grace and dignity, in a manner reminiscent of Cersei's agonising 'walk of shame' in *Game of Thrones*, thought to be inspired by the real-life justice meted out by Richard III to Jane Shore, a mistress of Edward IV. She is alone during her time at the gates of the palace, rejected by her family and friends and yet is able to draw on her own mental strength in order to survive. And not only does she survive, but she keeps her attitude positive, forgiving her oppressors and remaining unjaded. Strong to the core.

CHAPTER TWO

WARRIORS

Fighters, strategists and
bringers of justice

ARTEMIS

The archetypal woman who runs with the wolves, the assured, independent Artemis (Diana in Roman mythology) is at one with both nature and with her girlfriends.

From the very beginning, Artemis had a can-do attitude; minutes after being born, she pulled on a pair of gloves and, nine days later, helped her mother deliver her twin brother, Apollo. But then she was born to be a high achiever. Her father was Zeus, the King of the Gods and her mother, the beautiful Leto.

Artemis asserted her independence at an early age. In a poem written sometime in the second or third century BCE, Callimachus describes Artemis' third birthday party. When Zeus asks his daughter what she wants, the precocious toddler asks to be able to live without the distractions of love or marriage, to be given a bow and arrow, just like her brother's, to have a knee-length hunting costume for everyday wear and for sixty nine-year-old girls to be her choir and twenty more to help her care for her dogs. So far, so fairly reasonable. She also asks her father for all the

'Zeus has made you [Artemis] a lion
among women, and given you leave
to kill any at your pleasure . . . you
hunt down the ravening beasts in
the mountains and deer of the wilds.'

– HOMER, *THE ILIAD*

mountains on the planet and the job of bringing light to the world. Zeus roars with laughter – an indulgent father, he grants his daughter all of her wishes.

As Artemis grew older, she became renowned for her wild passion for nature; she captured six golden-horned deer to pull her chariot and practised hard with her bow. It might be difficult for modern readers to reconcile the goddess' love of animals with her hunting skills, but she killed only for food and punished those who killed pregnant animals for disturbing the balance of nature. She could be seen as the earliest grassroots environmentalist, a Jane Goodall or Dian Fossey, living on the ground, actively protecting vulnerable creatures. You see her trace in young environmental activists such as Greta Thunberg, the teenage Swedish climate activist who organised the first school strike for climate in 2019. Artemis' protection also extended to humans; she was the patron goddess of young girls, childbirth and midwifery.

LIVING THE DREAM

Despite living on Mount Olympus, Artemis didn't socialise with the other gods and avoided the politics and back-biting of the court, preferring to roam in the wild with her coterie of nymphs. It was a women-only commune straight out of a second-wave feminist fanzine. They hunted together, bathed in rivers and were fiercely protective of each other. Artemis was determined at all costs for them all to keep their virginity – a term that, at the time, referred more to marriage than chastity. Ovid tells the story of Actaeon who spied on the girl gang bathing naked. Artemis turned him into a stag, and his hounds tore him to pieces.

Artemis is said to have had female lovers, Cyrene, Atalanta and Anticleia, and she seems to have had a particularly close relationship with one of her band, Callisto. Ovid relates the story of how Zeus changed his appearance in order to resemble his daughter and attempted to seduce

Callisto. She started passionately kissing the person she believed to be Artemis, only to have that person transform into Zeus. After he raped her, she became pregnant. In an indication of just how far she was prepared to go in order to ensure her women remained dedicated to their Sapphic vows, when Artemis spotted her lover's swelling stomach, she became furious, expelling her from the collective. In some versions of the story, Callisto is transformed into a bear by Zeus; in others, his jealous wife, Hera, turns her into the animal; in others still, it is Artemis.

Artemis is believed to have had a hand in the death of Orion, her hunting partner and friendly rival. Accounts vary, some telling how she killed him after he attempted to rape her, others that her brother, Apollo, was jealous of her love for Orion and tricked his sister into killing him or sent a giant scorpion to despatch the god.

Artemis' gender-neutral dress sense, athletic good looks and representation of the plucky, determined heroine make her a favourite subject for sculptures and paintings. More commonly depicted in culture in her Roman Diana form, she appears in the opera *L'arbore Di Diana*, paintings by Titian and Rembrandt and in the seventeenth-century depiction of Diane de Poitiers, the powerful French lover of Henri II.

Whether as Artemis or Diana, the goddess continues to fascinate filmmakers and writers, too. You'll see direct, bow-toting descendants of the goddess in the *Hunger Games*' Katniss Everdee and *Brave*'s sparky Princess Merida. And it's not just those with literal bows in their hands who evoke her spirit – Lisbeth Salander, in Steig Larsson's *The Girl with the Dragon Tattoo*, and Dany, in *Game of Thrones*, are both Artemis archetypes. Her character resonates even more widely: at the funeral of British Princess Diana, in 1997, her brother invoked his sister's namesake saying she was, 'the most hunted person of the modern age'.

The hunting goddess' intense devotion to a life of freedom from her early years marks her out as someone special, even among deities. At three, she knew she wanted to hunt and devoted hours of practice to becoming the best, her arrows can be seen to represent her determination, focus and unwavering aim in her wider life. But perhaps her most striking attribute is her dedication to her sisters, girlfriends or workmates and their communal, outdoor lifestyle. What a time they must have had, outside of patriarchal Greek society, whooping and jumping in the open air – an all-female Utopia. Perhaps, in this age of smartphone addiction and twenty-four-hour news, we all need to hold tight to our own version of that dream.

ANATH

NORTHWEST SEMITIC:
GODDESS

Also known as
Anat
Antit
Anit
Anti
Anant

Need a friend who will leap to your defence? Look up Anath. This goddess of love and war takes loyalty to the extreme. Her passionate relationship with her beau Ba'al, or Hadad, also her brother, fuels her violent rampages – she loves hard, feels hard and fights hard.

Popular around 1000–1500 CE, Anath and her avatars were worshipped across Egypt and Canaan – modern-day Israel, Palestine, Lebanon, Syria and Jordan. She plays a major role in the fragmentary myths translated from the ancient Ugaritic texts, and even makes a brief cameo in the Hebrew Bible.

Her story is vividly described in the Ugaritic *Baal Cycle* (1400–1200 CE), pieced together from stone tablets found in Syria in 1958. Anath and her brother, Ba'al, were the offspring of El, the chief god (see Jezebel, pages 82–85). Ba'al was the lord of the sky, or 'Cloud Rider', commanding rainfall and thus the fertility of the country. We first meet Anath after Ba'al has successfully challenged the supremacy of sea god Yam, another son of El. Ba'al prepares a feast for

those still loyal to Yam, while Anath puts on her warpaint. Her hands are red with henna, hair braided, eyes heavy with liner and she's wearing her best clothes. She walks into the celebration, closes the doors purposefully behind her and slaughters her brother's enemies.

'Under her, like scattered balls, were heads; over her, like grasshoppers, were hands – soldiers' hands, piled up like locust swarms. She fastened heads onto her back; she girdled her waist with hands. Knee-deep, she plunged through warriors' blood – neck-deep through the soldiers' entrails. With a staff, she herded hostages, rabble-rousers with a bowstring.'

Impressive, if gory, and reminiscent of *Game Of Thrones*' Red Wedding in which guests were offered food, then slaughtered. Her belt garlanded with hands has echoes of Kālī's similarly gory accessory (see pages 72–75).

BURNING LOVE

Anath's 'maiden' title probably equates more closely to her youthful energy, independence and fierce spirit. She's frequently described as a virgin, but her appetite for sex was well-documented – she and her brother, Ba'al, transformed into a cow and bull to make love; in one story she bore him a calf and in another, they had seventy-seven children. Their relationship is fierce and intense. Ba'al messages Anath in no uncertain language:

> Let your feet run to me, let your legs race to me, for I have thoughts to tell you, and I have words to share: a thought of trees and a murmur of stone, a whisper between heaven and earth, between the deep and the stars. I understand the lightning beyond the heavens' ken, the thoughts beyond human knowledge, that which the throngs below cannot understand. Come, and I will show it: deep inside my mountain, holy Zaphon, in the sacred space on my native peak, in the paradise upon the hill of victory.

Anath's even hawkish when it comes to Ba'al's social standing. When El hummed and hawed about granting his son a palace, Anath stepped in, threatening: 'I shall surely drag him like a lamb to the ground, I shall make his grey hairs run with blood, the grey hairs of his beard thick with gore.' Anath is every 'don't mess with my man', claws-out soap star rolled into one violent goddess package.

She and Ba'al waged war with Mot, who symbolised drought and death. After many battles, Mot defeated and ate Ba'al, condemning him to the underworld. For seven years the earth was barren and crops failed. Only one woman could save the planet: Anath. She fomented revenge as she searched the netherworld 'like a cow for its calf' for the body of her brother and consort. When she found it, limp and lifeless, she buried him, making sacrifices and weeping. Her anger grew as she tracked Mot down. Her revenge was bloody, almost ritual: 'With a blade she cuts him; with the winnowing sieve she winnows him; with the fire she roasts him; with the mill she crushes him; in the fields she sows him, and the birds eat him'.

Ba'al later returned, the rains burst, and the land sprung to life again. Sadly, Mot was also resurrected. After an epic battle, Ba'al was declared as king.

Anath was described in other religions. In Egypt, she was worshipped as a war goddess: Ramesses II even made her his personal guardian and named his daughter and horse after her. She is thought to have been mentioned in the Hebrew Bible, and conflated with Athena in Greece. Although she and Ba'al were regarded in Canaanite myth as saviours, his name was later assumed for Beelzebub, and his horns associated with the devil. Anath was also often depicted with cattle horns.

ANATH TO THE RESCUE

Anath's story turns the protector trope on its head, gender-wise. In most stories, men are the guardians of women, fighting to free them from villains' evil clutches, searching for their lost loves, kissing them awake from deep sleeps.

For a goddess to decide that she is the woman to rescue her man – and in doing so save the world from drought and death – is quite a leap, even for modern audiences. And that she manages it in such spectacularly visceral fashion is yet another eye-opener. Anath is an independent thinker, a doer, all wrapped up in a brutally efficient killing machine.

DIVOKÁ ŠÁRKA

BOHEMIAN: WARRIOR

Also known as
Šárka

She sacrificed her dignity to win a battle. But did proto-radical feminist Divoká Šárka really finally fall for a man?

The story of the Maiden's War, the struggle between Czech men and women was said to have taken place in the fifth or sixth century CE. It was first documented in the eleventh century by Cosmas of Prague, a high-ranking cleric. It unravelled on the site of what is modern-day Prague, then a wild landscape, inhabited by several tribes.

Czech society was then matriarchal and ruled by Libuše, 'Queen of the Goths'. The youngest and wisest of King Krok's three daughters, she was gifted with seeing the future. She foretold that Prague, the city she had founded, would become a place where 'glory would touch the stars'. She used her predictive abilities to her advantage: when she fell in love with Přemysl, a ploughman, she reverse-engineered a vision in which her beloved became king. Under her leadership, the country prospered and women gained rights and privileges. However, when Libuše died, Přemysl took over as ruler and those rights were abruptly curtailed.

Czech women were furious at the matriarchal system coming to an end and a group of them declared war on men. This feud became bloody and lasted for hundreds of years. The women went on to be led by a fierce warrior, Vlasta, and her right-hand woman, Divoká Šárka. This story was first documented in the fourteenth-century *Dalimil Chronicle*. Their group of rebels created a radical separatist, women-only colony that sat across the Vltava River, near Vysehrad, a castle occupied by the patriarchal Premyslid dynasty. Divoká Šárka was tactically very clever. She realised that in order to defeat the men's army, the women's best chance was to kill their greatest warrior, Ctirad. So she came up with a plan. She organised a meeting with Ctirad in the place that later became known as the Divoká Šárka (Wild Sarka) valley.

'Šárka merely laughed; they all laughed and, wild with joy, they led their noble prisoner back to Děvín.'
– THE MAIDENS' WAR

There are two versions of ensuing events. In the first, Divoká Šárka got her friends to tie her naked to a tree and, as Ctirad and his men arrived, claimed that she had been captured by the band of women. In the other, she simply sat and waited for Ctirad. In both, however, she had bottles of mead stacked alongside her. She invited the warrior and his soldiers to drink the alcohol, passing them horn upon horn until they passed out. At this point, Divoká Šárka blew her hunting trumpet and a squad of women ran out from their hiding places in the forest and attacked the men. In some versions they killed them all, torturing and breaking Ctirad on a wheel; in others, they took the warrior prisoner.

The tactical manoeuvre paid off, for a while – the male army suffered from the loss of its best fighter. However, long-term, the women failed to win the war and the patriarchal, feudal system remained. Divoká Šárka refused to accept this and jumped to her death, from a cliff in the park – one of the rocky outcrops that is now known as Girl's Jump. In a less empowering version of the myth – the 1897 opera by Zdenek Fibich – she jumped because she had fallen in love with Ctirad.

The story of Divoká Šárka is dear to the Czech people. There is a school of thought that says the tale was inspired by ancient stories of female warriors from other cultures, while others believe that it sprang from the folk memory of the pagan matriarchal society that was around thousands of years before Christianity. What is possibly more important than its origins, however, is its value, at the end of the eighteenth century, to the Czech people as their language, nearly extinguished by Germany under Hapsburg rule, was rekindled. As Czechs became free from that rule, the focus of the tale also shifted: Vlasta and Divoká Šárka became less figures of fun and more figureheads for the burgeoning democratic movement. The new versions of the story by writers such as Alois Jirásek, writing before the First World War, were softened with a love interest and designed to appeal to women, the people who would read these stories of national pride to their children and hopefully raise a new generation of Czech nationalists.

At this point in history, the tale was also told in an epic poem by Jaroslav Vrchlický and another by Julius Zeyer, which formed the basis for the operas by Zdenek Fibich and Leoš Janáček. Romantic composer and national treasure Bedřich Smetana also dedicated a symphonic movement to the tale. The modern attempts to flesh out the character of Divoká Šárka caused tension in audiences, many of which saw the newly added suicide and resolution as falsifying the story for emotional resonance.

A WOMAN OF SUBSTANCE

The notion of a female-only enclave down the centuries must have been shocking to some, very appealing to others and yet fascinating to all. Amazon myths are common across cultures, but in this case, rather than the all-lady utopia being set in some far-off country, it was based in the same place in which the stories were told – Prague – making it close to home and within reach of contemporary readers.

Even in her original, stripped-down form, Divoká Šárka is an impressive character. She is cunning, combining battle tactics with womanly wiles to great effect. She is brave – stripped naked, tied to a tree to ensnare her enemy. And, even though the stories that tell how she fell in love with her prey have been dismissed as romantic whimsy, they show her as an appealingly fallible and real woman.

FREYJA

NORSE: GODDESS

Also known as
Freya
Freyia
Freja

Freyja's look is strong. She rides in a chariot pulled by cats, wearing fabulous jewellery and a cloak made from the feathers of a falcon slung over her shoulders. Her pet war pig is never far from her side. But it's not just her appearance that turns heads. The Norse goddess of love, fertility, battle and death, is famed for her skills in the occult, her articulacy, nimble word play and bravery.

A member of the Vanir tribe of wise gods, Freyja's father was Njord; her mother was thought to be Nerthus, Njord's sister. As goddess of battle and death, Freyja picked soldiers who'd died in battle to live in her afterlife hall, Folkvangr, while the rest went to Odin's Valhalla.

Married to obscure god Od, a pairing almost exactly mirrored by husband-and-wife-god-team Frigg and Odin, many believe that Freyja and Frigg are, at root, the same goddess. Od and Freyja have two daughters, Hnoss and Gersemi. Her bond with Od is strong. When he's away voyaging and pillaging – as a Viking

god, that happens frequently – she misses him desperately, crying tears that turn to gold, convenient for a jewellery-loving goddess. However, her anguish doesn't extend to remaining faithful to him; while he's at sea, she sleeps with slaves and warriors, including Ottar, who she ends up turning into an enchanted boar. Loki, the sly god, taunts her about her lustful nature when he turns up to a feast, spoiling for a fight and a little drunk. He accuses her, via a 'flyting' (a poem in old Norse), of sleeping with every elf and god in the hall, then the two spar verbally. Freyja accuses Loki of lying, exclaiming, 'Mad art thou, Loki! In recounting thy foul misdeeds.' In return, he accuses her of bedding her brother, prompting the other gods to chime in to defend her. In this heated exchange, we get a glimpse of Freyja's bravery and sparky wit.

A HEDONISTIC GODDESS

As well as her wisdom, her bravery and her love of carnal delights, Freyja has a reputation as a materialistic goddess who loves her home comforts. Her bedroom is beautiful, but impregnable without her permission, while her most precious possession is the Brisingamen, a necklace of incredible beauty. However, she had to work hard to get and keep it.

Out walking one frosty morning, Freyja happened on a cave. On entering it, she saw four dwarves creating a piece of gold jewellery so beautiful she instantly became obsessed. But no matter how much silver and gold she offered them, the dwarves refused to sell it to her – they would only give up the necklace if Freyja spent a night with each of them. Freyja agreed and, after four nights of passion with the tiny silversmiths, she took it home. Little did she know that her old friend, Loki, had been watching. Always keen to stir up trouble, he ran to Odin and told him of Freyja's wanton activities. Odin spotted an opportunity to grab the precious item for himself and commanded Loki to steal it. Loki turned himself into a fly, squeezed through a tiny gap into Freyja's locked bedroom and stole the necklace from around her neck. When Freyja awoke, she was furious and, true to her bold style, immediately confronted Odin who told her that she could only have her precious trinket back if she agreed to stir up hatred and warfare across the land. Freyja agreed.

Freyja was much more than a collector of expensive objects. She was a powerful sorceress, using her falcon feather cloak to fly across the night sky and practising magic. The Norse people regarded magic as a feminine power and Freyja became its poster girl. She was revered by the *völvur* – travelling women who used spells and chants to foretell the future or to curse enemies. She was also called upon by women in childbirth to protect the mother and baby.

Freyja was a tenacious goddess; not only was she the last living deity, sacrificing dutifully even after her friends and family were long gone, but Freyja worship continued down the centuries, even as Christianity usurped the old religions. Although her character was besmirched by the incomers and her beloved poetry banned, she continued to be venerated by women in fertility rituals. There are still many places across Scandinavia with names derived from hers and she was regarded a symbol of romantic love even into the early twentieth century. Her likeness is captured in poems and paintings and she even makes a cameo appearance in Denmark's national anthem. It's thought that the story of Snow White and the Seven Dwarves may have its roots in the tale of how Freyja won her necklace. Which puts a *whole* new spin on the tale.

Freyja isn't a traditional warrior goddess, roaring into battle; her courage is revealed through her assertiveness. She's smart and quick-witted, a woman thumbing her nose at sexual norms. Yet she feels deeply – those golden tears – and has mastered powerful magic. This blend of hedonism, fallability, wisdom and bravery makes her feel modern thousands of years after she was thought to have existed, and her unusual story serves to inspire the women of Scandinavia and beyond to this day.

THE FURIES

ROMAN/GREEK:
GODDESSES

Also known as
The Erinyes
The Erinys

Their name may summon images of beasts boiling with hatred, but it was the Furies' icily targeted justice that had murderers, bigamists and thieves looking uneasily over their shoulders. Their carefully meted, tough retaliation remains an inspiration for activists and agents for social change today.

Even among the gods of ancient Greece, the Furies were regarded as ancient spirits. Hesiod's *Theogony* told how the grisly looking creatures had their origins in a violent act: the castration of Uranus by his son, Cronus. The latter threw his father's testicles into the sea and as the drops of blood sprang to life, the Furies were born.

Usually described as a trio, the three sisters lived in Tartarus, a fiery abyss in the Underworld. The siblings have been variously described as having hair and belts writhing with snakes, eyes that dripped gore, with leathery bat wings sprouting from their backs and bodies blackened and cracked like charcoal. They carried brass scourges or serpent-shaped whips. Their powers included immortality, superhuman strength, flight and the ability to breathe poisons, but most of all they were famed for their unremitting avenging of what they deemed to be transgressions. Mortals would deliver their grievances to the Furies via curses and the three would pursue the perpetrators relentlessly, whipping them into a hideous death, often driving them to insanity. They were particularly fond of punishing those who had violated familial ties, but could also turn their wrath on an entire nation-state, condemning it to disease and famine.

The Furies are the antecedents of more witchy triple acts – The Fates are close relatives, while Morrígan (see pages 90–93) and Shakespeare's Weird Sisters bear a striking resemblance. Like ancient, twisted Spice Girls, each member of the Furies had a name laden with meaning. Alecto, or 'unceasing anger', was in charge of moral crimes, driving perpetrators to madness. Her sister, Megaera, the 'jealous one', punished those who committed adultery and has often been portrayed as the archetypal shrew. Ovid's *Metamorphoses* describes the third sister, Tisiphone, the 'blood avenger', as wearing 'a robe all red with dripping gore and wound a snake about her waist'. She chased down those who committed murder, patricide, homicide and fratricide. In Statius' *Thebaid*, she incites Aeolian hero Tydeus to cannibalism, goading him into madness and driving him to devour the brain of his enemy, Melanippus.

Although the Furies have became a byword for rage, early descriptions were more subtle. Yes, they doled out severe punishment, but they were the embodiment of the 'firm but fair' maxim. Righteous, purposeful, with cool anger, but able to manage that ire and use it to fuel their retribution, they possessed a finely tuned moral compass, punishing humans who transgressed mortal rules. A masterclass in channelling emotions into a form of positive result, Alecto, Megaera and Tisiphone were cold reason and iron will incarnate.

The three judges reached a peak in Aeschylus' Oresteia trilogy. Goaded by the vengeful ghost of Clytemnestra – who, with her lover, had murdered her husband, Agamemnon – they rose up from the Underworld in order to hunt down her killer, her son Orestes, who had acted out of revenge for his father's death. They pursued the boy, whispering and chanting: 'We drive matricides from their homes. We are called Curses in our home below the earth.' Luckily for Orestes, Athena persuaded his stalkers to let him stand trial by jury; Orestes was acquitted and the Furies became goddesses-in-residence in Athens as they are transformed into the Eumenides, or 'kindly ones'.

'Dark-coloured queens, whose glittering eyes are bright with dreadful, radiant, life-destroying light: eternal rulers, terrible and strong, to whom revenge and tortures dire belong.'
- ORPHIC HYMN 70

COOL JUSTICE

The first half of the story shines a light on the internal workings of the sisters. At heart they work to their own frame of rules, and, although vengeful, never lose their composure. They believe in justice above all. However, Aeschylus' Athena undermines them. Some see their 'kindly ones' rebrand as cynical, a signal that the trio have been disempowered by Athena, their fire quenched. Others see it as a euphemistic pseudonym, used to aid fearful people hoping to avoid referring to them directly, and still more believe that this symbolised the way the old punishments of the goddesses were cleverly integrated into a more modern justice system.

Anger is a vital element in social change and progression, a motivation for political action, but women who display it are often condemned as irrational. Through the centuries, girls have been told that it is unladylike to be angry. The Furies lay waste to this stereotype, defiantly unrepentant about their dedication to justice.

We see their legacy in the righteous, controlled rage of Sojourner Truth's wry nineteenth-century anti-slavery speeches, in Austrian Holocaust survivor Simon Wiesenthal's dogged pursuit of Nazis, in tennis legend Billie Jean King coolly thrashing Bobby Riggs in the 1970s' 'Battle of the Sexes' match and in the measured but simmering addresses of the pupils who, in 2018, saw their friends gunned down at the Marjory Stoneman Douglas High School in Parkland, Florida. The bearing and response of the Furies is something truly intimidating on which to draw.

CIHUATETEO

In Aztec culture, women who perished in childbirth became Cihuateteo, spirits. Their sacrifice was respected as deeply as that of warriors who'd fallen in combat, their job, to guard the sun as it set.

In contrast to most cultures' nurturing, peaceful take on childbirth, Aztecs viewed labour as a war. Pregnant women were warriors, readied to take on a bloody battle by their sergeants-at-arms, midwives, who prepared them for motherhood in a series of sweat bath rituals. This acceptance of, and preparation for, the visceral process of childbirth was a realistic view – these mothers didn't bring a child into the world smilingly and serene, they fought hard to keep the baby and themselves alive and healthy. Some historians have even argued that motherhood was established as the blueprint for bravery before Meso-American society required fighters.

Women who died during childbirth were considered to be casualties of combat and honoured accordingly. A funeral party that included the woman's

'Women who died in childbirth were considered to be casualties of war. A funeral party ... would carry the body, now regarded as divine, to a location dedicated to goddesses.'

husband, her midwife and a coterie of female elders armed with swords and shields would carry the body, now regarded as divine, to a location dedicated to goddesses. There, the corpse would be fiercely defended against looters – the middle finger of the left hand and the hair of the dead woman, it was believed, were totems that would make warriors invincible and blind their enemies.

After four days, the spirit of the woman would ascend to heaven. In Aztec culture, your place in the afterlife was governed by the manner in which you died, rather than your deeds and achievements. The Cihuateteo lived in a dark place in the sky called Cihuatlampa ('Place of Women') and their role balanced that of the spirits of male fighters. The men guarded the sun in the morning and early afternoon; the women who'd died in childbirth at sundown. This was the highest possible honour in the Aztec belief system, the women accompanying the sun as it set, singing it lullabies as they would to their own children. These heavenly rewards served as incentives to become mothers, and for both men and women to become warriors, to die in battle for the good of the community.

However, there was a darker twist to the tale, in the Cihuateteo's return to earth every fifty-two days. Their appearance for these revisits was terrifying; they had gaunt skeleton faces and hands like gnarled eagle claws. Garlanded with skulls and wearing horned headdresses, bare-breasted, with belts – sometimes made from two-headed snakes – slung around their hips and long hair cascading down their backs, they made an intimidating sight. According to Spanish chroniclers of Meso-American traditions, who regarded the society they'd conquered as subhuman, the Cihuateteo haunted crossroads. At these junctions, such writers warned, the Cihuateteo would hunt for children, who they'd leave paralysed and diseased or steal away, leaving only a knife in their place. Crossroads became associated with death and evil, as a result. The Cihuateteo were also said to inflict sickness on men, palsy, mental illnesses and also to incite them to commit adultery.

The Aztecs were said to have attempted to appease their avenging spirits by creating shrines at the crossroads, decorated with cut paper and colourful blooms and piled high with offerings such as toasted corn, tamales and bread shaped like butterflies. Children were kept inside on the nights they were due to descend, kept safe from the claws of these demons who ached to hold their earthly children.

CHANGING THE STORY

It is interesting to note that this terrifying take on the Cihuateteo's return to earth was that of the Spanish colonisers. Previously the Cihuateteo had simply been honoured warriors, a testament to the importance of women in Aztec society as strong maternal figures.

The Cihuateteo myth can be seen to reflect the conflict of modern attitudes to childbirth: should women keep their composure and silent reverence while in labour, or should they shout and fight? The pressure valve release of the Cihuateteo returning to earth regularly to vent their rage at losing a child or wreak revenge can even be viewed as a mourning ritual. A way of releasing emotions, of allowing women to mark their loss.

KĀLĪ

HINDU: GODDESS

Also known as
Kālikā
Shyāmā

Kālī knows how to make a dramatic entrance. The first recorded description of this Hindu goddess, in the Devi Mahatmya, c. 600 CE, is incandescent; she emerges from the forehead of the goddess Durga, fully formed; a sunken-cheeked crone with four arms, coloured black, dressed in animal skins and carrying a skull-topped staff.

Born of Durga's anger, Kālī is immediate in her reputation as the black-hued goddess of death, rapidly despatching the demons her progenitor is fighting. Later in the battle, Durga beckons her to help slay the demon Raktabija. Each time a drop of his blood touches the earth, another foe springs up so that, in order to put a halt to the thousands of demons, Kālī licks up the gore.

In one telling, she gets high on blood and rampages around the battlefield, tearing apart and devouring every demon in sight and gleefully decorating herself with the limbs and entrails of her victims. The god Shiva – in some traditions, the Supreme Being, in

others the destroyer – is horrified, and throws himself under her feet. This shocks the goddess into calming down. Thus, Kālī is often portrayed standing on Shiva with her tongue sticking out.

AN EMPOWERING GODDESS

In other origin stories, Kālī acts as the dark, assertive yin to the protector goddess Parvati's more compliant, sunny yang; both are consorts of Shiva. When Shiva asks Parvati to help him slay the demon Daruka, who can only be killed by a woman, she manifests as Kālī, drawing on the goddess' power and rage. In an age and tradition in which subservience and modesty were prized in women, perhaps Kālī acted as a totem of fury, the goddess to be invoked when women needed to draw on their anger for strength. Parvati couldn't be seen to be battle hungry; she had to summon Kālī in order to fight.

Kālī is a fierce role model. Even her basic look is intimidating, from her sharp teeth to her raging eyes, but then she piles on the gruesome accessories; adornments made from the remnants of her victims: a belt hung with arms, a necklace made of skulls, earrings of bones. She manifests in either her four- or ten-armed form, with blue or black skin, her hair wild, her tongue flickering out of her fanged mouth. In one arm she carries a sword, in the other a decapitated head. Some may have been inspired to take this bravado too far – the Thuggee sect of the fourteenth to nineteenth centuries were believed to have considered themselves children of Kālī, and carried out ritualistic assassinations in her name, robbing and strangling their victims. However, some scholars believe English colonialists overstated the violence of the cult in order to justify the British's increased presence in the territory.

Her appearance is, of course, deeply symbolic – many regard the sawn-off head as representing the human ego, the sword enlightenment and Kālī as liberating her children from their earthly delusion. Somewhere around the seventeenth century she was rebranded courtesy of tantric poets, her fierce black complexion was softened to blue, her face became

> 'Dancing mad with joy. Come mother, come! For terror is thy name, death is in thy breath, and every shaking breath, destroys a world fore'r.'
> – SWAMI VIVEKANANDA

youthful and she smiled. In yet another interpretation by the tantric strand of Hinduism, Kālī is referred to as the 'Divine Mother'. Devouring yet benevolent, she shows that the beauty of life is counterbalanced by the reality of death, yet is fiercely protective of her beloved children. She embodies feminine energy and fertility. Those female-centric concepts became elevated to the extent that a number of Hindu societies who worshipped the goddess were matrilineal – wealth passed from mother to daughter. She is still wildly popular – with over 750 million followers, Hinduism is the third biggest religion and way of life in the world. In the Shaktism form of Hinduism, she is worshipped as one of the Mahavidya, the ten aspects of Adi Parashakti, forms of the goddess Parvati.

THE MANY FACES OF KĀLĪ

In tantric Hindu traditions, Kālī has a more philosophical symbolism, embodying time rather than pure destruction. As she marks the ticking of the seconds, she consumes all things; everyone must eventually bow to her. She stands or dances on her bedrock and companion Shiva, spinning the wheels of creation, birth, growth, death. This interpretation is interesting: Kālī symbolises the relentlessness cruelty of years passing. She is inescapable – cruel, even – but a reality check. Our faces will inevitably become bone, and when they do, Kālī will add them to her grim necklace. Death is our common fate, but it's helpful to be philosophical about it.

The subtle differences in the various versions of Kālī can cause some confusion. And the veneration of such an outwardly fierce, terrifying goddess may not make sense immediately. The nineteenth-century Bengali saint Ramakrishna once asked a follower why he continued to worship Kālī. The man replied, 'Maharaj, when they are in trouble your devotees come running to you. But, where do you run when you are in trouble?' Kālī can be seen as hired muscle, the girl you turn to when you feel a fight brewing – her devotion to her followers and friends is fierce. When she battles alongside her allies, she is unstoppable, while on a more personal level, she conjures up the righteous anger we need in order to vanquish our demons, both inner and in the real world. So, the next time you need a shot of courage, perhaps close your eyes and think, 'What would Kālī do?'

YENNENGA

MOSSI, AFRICAN: PRINCESS   The legend of Yennenga, the warrior princess who helped found a kingdom, has been told and kept alive in oral tradition for over 900 years. There are many variations on the story, which is based on a real historical figure, but all agree that this strong-willed, strong-armed woman made an impact that still reverberates in Burkina Faso, western Africa.

In the fourteenth or fifteenth century, Yennenga lived in the Dagomba Kingdom (now northern Ghana) with her father, King Nedega, and siblings. Her three brothers each commanded their own battalion and she was determined to match their prowess in battle. Her father encouraged her to learn horse riding, fighting, spear-throwing and bowmanship and she was a natural. These abilities, combined with her height and muscular frame, made her a formidable opponent; she won many victories for her father's army and became commander of her own. Nicknamed 'The Svelte', she wore fatigues and armour and was often mistaken for a man as she led her troops into skirmishes.

She gained a reputation as someone who inspired devotion in her fighters and worked political marvels in new territories.

Yennenga's father was very protective of her, yet valued his daughter as a warrior – she was a vital cog in his battle machine. So much so, that when she asked if she might have some time to relax, find love, perhaps even marry and raise a family, he refused. Yennenga respected her father, so returned to fighting for a few years, but, like any teenager, yearned to be like her friends and speak to boys. She asked if she might have some time off, but again her father wouldn't countenance it.

Angry, and determined to show her father her strong feelings through actions rather than words, Yennenga planted a field of okra. The plants prospered, but she let them die and rot away. When her father asked her why she had wasted the crop, she replied angrily, 'This field looks like how I feel. Here I am, my ovaries withering and dying, my soul crying out for someone, and you don't care.'

However – even though he was the one who'd been so keen for her to be brave and strong – her dad wasn't so impressed by her stubbornness. Worried that his daughter would disobey him, he locked her up. Grounded. Of course, the battle-cunning Yennenga soon hatched a plan and, with the help of one of her father's guards, disguised herself as a man and broke out of her prison. She rode fast through the night, across rivers, through the forests. Eventually, in the north of the region, both she and her horse tired.

A NEW LIFE

Almost passing out through fatigue, Yennenga met Riale, a solitary but famous elephant hunter. He initially thought she was male and asked her to stay with him while she recovered. His guest's spear-throwing and riding abilities impressed him and when Yennenga's helmet tumbled off revealing that she was a woman, he fell hopelessly in love with her. The pair became a formidable team: Riale taught her how to hunt, while Yennenga showed him her strategy skills. In time, they married and added a son to their team, Ouedraogo, named after the horse on which his mother had escaped his grandfather.

When Ouedraogo was 15, the family visited grandfather Nedega. The king had had time to reflect on his daughter's actions and had grown more mellow in his old age. Eventually, he welcomed his new family and gave his grandson gifts – horses, cows and some of his best fighters. Ouedraogo took these presents and used them wisely. He conquered the Boussansi tribes, later marrying and founding the city of Tenkodogo and the Mossi Kingdom. His sons went on to become important leaders, forging alliances and building on his success. Their tribe, the Mossi, dominated the region of the Upper Volta River for hundreds of years, and still consider Yennenga to be the mother of their people. Statues of

'Whether women choose
to have a partner and family
is a personal issue, but
the right for them to do
so should be absolute.'

her dot the streets of Burkino Faso and football teams and awards are named after her horse.

Yennenga is a powerful representation of womanhood – not just athletic and beautiful, but with a maternal urge so strong that she defied her family and beloved father to fulfil it. Her experience sums up many of the dilemmas facing women today – the push and pull between career and children and the central question of do we really want children and, if so, when?

While men seemingly have their whole lives to reproduce, for women the biological clock and the whispering of what society deems acceptable grows louder with each period. The story of Yennenga flips historical gender stereotypes on their head and so is a parable fit for a more modern age. This is a princess torn between the wishes of her family, her glittering career in battle and her own desire to become a mother, something that many women today will achingly identify with.

Yennenga not only had battle bravery, but was smart, too – defying her father and running away, knowing that she was compelled to do this. She needed to explore her maternal side and fall in love. Whether women choose to have a partner and family is a personal issue, but the right for them to do it should be absolute. Thousands of years ago, this teenage princess knew that and made huge sacrifices in order to fulfil her personal ambitions.

JEZEBEL

HEBREW/CHRISTIAN:
QUEEN

Also known as
Jezabel

Jezebel's name has become a cipher for wanton, wicked women, but the evidence is that she was a lot more complex, powerful and strong-willed than her cartoonish reduction. This ninth-century and Hebrew Bible (Old Testament) queen was at the epicentre of the war between followers of the old gods and those of Yahweh (God). However, despite a malicious campaign waged against Jezebel, her profound influence and incredible character couldn't be concealed.

As the privileged daughter of priest and king, Ethbaal, Jezebel was an educated, politically aware woman. She was brought up in modern-day Lebanon as a worshipper of, among other gods, Ba'al (see Anath, pages 52–55). Ba'al was later depicted by Christian scribes as the devil, represented by the horns of a bull, but at this time he was a bounteous god of rain and fertility. Jezebel married King Ahab of the northern kingdom of Israel, moving to his country along with 850 of her priests. This union would have been political, a strategic alliance of families, but there was a major hurdle to overcome: the people of Israel worshipped Yahweh, the Jewish god, an incarnation of the modern Christian God.

Ahab was reasonable, however. He not only tolerated Jezebel's worship, but built her an altar to Ba'al. This wasn't well received by the country's prophets and religious bigwigs. They were inflamed further when Jezebel started killing followers of Yahweh. The prophet Elijah was furious and challenged Jezebel's priests to a duel. They met on Mount Carmel, their task to slaughter a bull, then set it on fire, with no torch or match. The Ba'al priests started to dance and cut themselves. They prayed for hours, but the pyre remained unlit. Elijah then took to the oche. He sprinkled what looked like water on his bull, called on God and, near-instantly, the beast burst into flames. The battle was over. In shockingly cold retribution, Elijah slaughtered all of Jezebel's men.

> 'My grandfather was a Pentecostal preacher. It was a sin to even pluck your eyebrows, and they thought it was a sin for me to be there looking like Jezebel.'
> – DOLLY PARTON

The queen was furious and, in a dramatic, bold move, established herself as her enemy's equal, by saying: 'If you are Elijah, so I am Jezebel.' She threatened Elijah: 'Thus and more may the gods do if by this time tomorrow I have not made you like one of them.' Unlike many women in the Bible, Jezebel had a voice, a powerful, agile, sarcastic one at that. Elijah fled in terror at her vicious promise, hiding out at Mount Sinai.

THE ADVENTURES OF JEZEBEL

Next, Jezebel annexed a vineyard for her husband. Ahab had been sulking; a man named Naboth refused to give him his land to make into a vegetable garden. Jezebel sprang into action, writing inflammatory letters to the elders of Jezreel, Naboth's city, that told of his blasphemy of his God and king. Furious and riled enough to become a boulder-toting mob, the townspeople stoned Naboth to death. Elijah saw this as a chance to reappear and threatened Ahab, telling him that his family would die in Jezreel, their bones eaten by dogs and picked clean by birds.

A few years later, Ahab died in battle with the Syrians. Accounts vary, but the 2 Kings book of the Bible tells how, after the death of Jezebel's son Ahaziah, his younger brother – Joram – became king. During this time, Elijah's successor, Elisha, had continued his predecessor's crusade. He declared his military wingman, Jehu, to be the true king of Israel, thus sparking a civil war. Jehu and Joram met on the battlefield, where Jehu heaped insults upon Jezebel, calling her a whore and a witch; he then slaughtered the king. However, he had to kill the queen, too, in order to assume the throne, a testament to Jezebel's true power.

The drama intensified. Jezebel got word that Jehu was on the warpath, and driving his chariot to her palace. Astute enough to realise that he must slaughter her in order to achieve his ambitions, Jezebel calmly sat at her dressing table. She put on make-up, combed and styled her hair, waiting for the inevitable. This was perhaps the queen's finest hour: she knew she was about to be killed, but she chose to face her fate with dignity, in a way worthy of her position. As she sat high in her tower, she was ultimately in control. Leaning out of her window, in a last display of defiance she insulted Jehu who, in turn, ordered Jezebel's servant eunuchs to throw her out of the window. They complied. Her bloodied body lay on the pavement below, picked over by dogs.

As a result of Jehu's taunting of Joram, and Jezebel's determination to wear lipstick to the last, 'Jezebel' became a byword for wantonness. This insult reverberated through history; at a particularly low point in the nineteenth century, African women slaves were labelled by white society as 'Jezebels' or temptresses, a repellent and weak excuse for their rape by their slave owners. Her reputation soaked through to popular culture, too: 'Jezebel' by musician Frankie Laine tells the story of a girl 'made to torment man' by the devil, and the iconic Bette Davis starred in a film of the same name as a strong-willed Southern belle. Even writer Margaret Atwood's *The Handmaid's Tale* has a brothel called Jezebel's, with prostitutes similarly named. However, latterly our Jezebel's reputation has started to be reclaimed, most notably by online feminist magazine *Jezebel*, and also by writers such as Lesley Hazleton, author of a revisionist biography of the biblical queen.

Jezebel is an extraordinary character. Transposed into an alien culture at a young age, she remains outspoken, politically savvy and determined to maintain her cultural and religious identity. Despite her husband's weaknesses, she is dedicated to him and to his position; there are clear clues that she is the true power behind the throne. Although she has since been cast as a harlot, there is no evidence for her adultery in the Bible. Many scholars claim that her reputed 'whoredom' refers to her worshipping multiple gods; others that priestesses were often recast, misogynistically, as prostitutes. For Christian revisionist writers, Jezebel not only represented women having power, a voice, an opinion, but she embodied the old religion. To secure the worship of the newer god, Yahweh, Jezebel not only had to be killed, but her reputation besmirched, her name dragged through the dust just as her body had been by the pack of dogs. That her determined, articulate character still shines through is testament to what an incredible, strong woman Jezebel must have been.

CHAPTER THREE

BRINGERS OF MISFORTUNE

Destructors, havoc-wreakers,
harbingers of doom

HEL

Often sketched as an archetypal chariot-riding, savage-hound-owning, maleficent goddess – after all, she did give her name to what we now know as Hell – this Norse deity had a more rational purpose, representing the finite nature of mortal life.

According to the *Prose Edda*, written by the thirteenth-century Icelandic scholar Snorri Sturluson, Hel's father was Loki, the perennially annoying trickster god, her mother, the giantess Angrboda and her brothers, Fenrir the wolf and Jormungand, the giant serpent whose huge body went on to encircle Midgard, the visible world. The family made their home in Jötunheimr, the Norse land of the giants.

Many prophecies were made about Hel and her brothers, none good, so Odin sent his gods to bring the rag-tag siblings to him. Throwing the serpent into the sea, he kept the wolf (until he could control him no longer) and Hel was cast into a part of the Underworld called Niflheim, renamed Hel in her honour.

THE JOURNEY TO HEL

Hel has been described as half-alive, half dead, half-flesh coloured, half-dark blue and is frequently depicted as a semi-skeleton. Sturluson wrote of her: 'Her hall is called Sleet-Cold; her dish, Hunger; Famine is her knife; Idler, her thrall; Sloven, her maidservant; Pit of Stumbling, her threshold, by which one enters; Disease, her bed; Gleaming Bale (bleak misfortune), her bed-hangings.' He also recounted that her kingdom, Hel, was a place of slush, ice and snow, where those who were dishonourable and died a 'straw death' – not in battle – would spend eternity.

> 'Her hall is called Sleet-Cold; her dish, Hunger; Famine is her knife; Idler, her thrall; Sloven, her maidservant; . . . Disease, her bed.'
> – STURLUSON, *PROSE EDDA*

The journey to this place was given great importance in Sturluson's account. On perishing, first you'd navigate Helveg, a rocky road, before being confronted with a giantess named Móðguðr – the furious battler – and then Garmr, Hel's bloodstained guard dog, who looked fierce, but could be appeased with a Hel-cake. Hel's kingdom was said to consist of many huge mansions, each staffed by numerous servants. In early stories, it is not as bleak a place; those who had lived good lives found peace there. In some sagas, however, Hel took a more active role and would go out to reap the dead, riding a three-legged, white horse and using a rake or a broom.

The *Prose Edda* also tells the story of the death of the god Baldr, beloved son of Odin and Frigg. Baldr had had a traditional viking boat burial and had made his final journey to Hel. Hermóðr – son of Odin and messenger of the gods – volunteered to ride to Hel to bring Baldr back to Asgard, the home of the gods. When he got there, Hermóðr told Hel how the gods had wept themselves dry for Baldr, but the goddess was cold and merciless, demanding that every last being must weep, alive or dead, before he be allowed to return to the kingdom of the living. When the troll Þokk (thought to be Loki in disguise) refused to shed a tear, Baldr was condemned to eternity in Hel. Later, the story predicted how, at the final cycle of battles, known as Ragnarök, Hel would raise a vast, creaking army of the dead to fight alongside her father Loki.

Hel, with her half-rotting face and corpse army, provides rich pickings for pop culture. It's thought that her appearance inspired the mask of the harlequin, who appeared in the performances of *Commedia dell'arte*, a theatrical form that flourished in late sixteenth-century Europe. More recently, the TV show *Game of Thrones* cherry-picked aspects of her story, while she also plays a major role in Marvel's film *Thor: Ragnarok*, as 'Hela', brought to life by actress Cate Blanchett. She is, unsurprisingly, a poster girl for Scandinavian metal bands and the lyrics of Amon Amarth's 'Hel' are largely based upon Snorri's gruesome description of her.

Latterly, it has been suggested that Hel was not always such a clear-cut villain, and that Snorri's account may have been an attempt to integrate the old religion with the new Christianity. Old Norse sources are a little more ambivalent about her kingdom and the nature of Hel – they didn't particularly regard it as a place where souls suffered, but as somewhere life continued, much as it did in the mortal world. Across Europe, her close relations, Holle and Hulda (see Berchta, pages 34–37), appeared more actively munificent, mother goddesses, bound into agriculture and home life. Hel is the goddess of death and the afterlife, but in the context of the natural order of things, rather than a deity bringing early destruction or misfortune.

Hel personifies the 'crone' in the maiden–mother–crone triple goddess common to many religions. The crone signifies the final chapter of life, the dark before the dawn, and must die in order for the maiden to live and the cycle to restart. For there to be growth, there must also be death and decay. Her depiction as one-part rotting corpse is an indication of her straight-talking approach to death. She is a shepherdess of death, providing a safe haven for those who haven't died in a 'noble' fashion, keeping their souls. Sadly for Hel, this brutal honesty has, down the centuries, simplified into a one-note representation of evil.

MORRÍGAN

CELTIC: GODDESS

Also known as
Morrígu
Mór-Ríoghain

Is Morrígan the singular queen of the Tuatha Dé Danaan, part of Ireland's race of supernatural beings? Or a reprobate girl gang? Whichever, trouble is always rumbling in the dust near this warmongering, shape-shifting goddess, whose favourite form is that of the crow and who set the template for goth girls down the centuries.

Morrígan's story is soaked in gore. She is a warmonger, giving strength to her people by driving them into the frenzy required for battle. Her bloodlust sees her encouraging opposite sides in battle, throwing thunderbolt spells of battle magic, dancing on swords and spear points, cackling and whipping soldiers into the frenzy needed for victory.

However, there is more to her than a violent cheerleader. Irish mythology has a track record of splitting its deities into threes: the land goddesses of Ireland, the three craftsmen gods and the three gods of skill. In the rich mythology of Ireland, there are up to five aspects of Morrígan that can form a trio, but the three most common are Badb, who transforms into a

crow as a warning of impending conflict, soaring over battlefields, croaking her prophecies. She would join in battles in her female form, confusing troops. She also acted as a psychopomp – accompanying soldier's dead souls to the next world. Macha was deeply connected to the land, the soil, its crops, its families and its wealth, and was concerned with the well-being of the Irish nation. She was seen as a kingmaker, bestowing sovereignty. She was a runner, once winning a race against horses while heavily pregnant. After her victory, she gave birth to twins, then died, cursing the men of Ulster to have childbirth pains whenever war was near. Annan, was the third, a gentler sister, associated with fertility and cattle, who would winnow out the weakest soldiers on the battlefield, comforting them in death. Some contemporary writers substitute the battle-furious Nemain for this gentle aspect.

'Over his head is shrieking
A lean hag, quickly hopping
Over the points of the
weapons and shields;
She is the grey-haired Morrigii.'
– POEM COMMEMORATING THE
BATTLE OF MAGH RATH

TALES OF MORRÍGAN

The first mention of Morrígan is in the eighth century, her name used in Latin manuscripts as a generic term for a female monster. However, her first outing as a solo entity is in the *Ulster Cycle* of Celtic mythology, a series of seventh and eighth century poems anthologised from the twelfth to fifteenth centuries. Believed to be set in the first century CE, these scripts tell of her relationship with Cú Chulainn, a young boy and one of the most famous of Irish mythological heroes. It's that old story; boy meets girl, girl offers him sex, boy refuses, girl reveals herself to be an unfeasibly powerful war goddess. After Cú rejects her advances, Morrígan becomes angry, determined to wreak her revenge, transforming into an eel, a wolf and a cow, but is outwitted and defeated by Cú. Finally, she transforms into an old woman milking a cow and tricks him into healing her.

Morrígan went on to appear again to Cú, this time, ominously as a woman washing bloody armour in a stream, a bad portent. Many years later, Cú was mortally wounded in battle and tied himself to a boulder with his own innards in order to die a hero, on his feet. His death was marked by a crow landing on his shoulder – a final goodbye from his nemesis, Morrígan, perhaps?

In the *Cath Maige Tuired*, believed to have been written in the sixth to tenth centuries, but preserved only in a sixteenth-century manuscript, Morrígan is seductive. She invites the Dagda, a Tuatha Dé Danaan chief and fertility god, to have sex with her in a pre-battle ritual on the Samhain. This was one of the most important Celtic festivals, a time when cattle were brought down from the hills, and the people prepared for the winter. Perhaps this union of the bounteous, life-filled Dagda and the death-obsessed Morrígan, was symbolic of the summer giving way to leaner, colder times. After the coupling, the Dagda went to war, where he witnessed the power of the goddess' spells; her screeched poems helped drive his foes into the sea. The battle ended with Morrígan foretelling the end of the world, while scooping up handfuls of the slain king's blood to give back to the river where their tryst had taken place.

The story of Morrígan emerged at a muddy, bloody point in her country's history. Old Ireland was a place of tribal grudges, cattle raiding and churning politics. Brute strength in war was essential, so having a fearsome battle goddess on your side would have been an essential bolster. Stories of this fierce woman were shouted at pre-battle rallies, giving the young, frightened soldiers strength on which to draw, whipping them into a fight-ready frenzy.

Her sexy, tough image has also made the Morrígan a staple of popular culture; a rich seam to mine for black metal lyrics, a game character who will appeal to boys and girls and regularly appears in fantasy fiction. Scratch a little deeper, though, and she's more than a pout, a crow and a spear. She is multifaceted, reminding us that light and dark are both part of the ebb and flow of life. Her wielding of chaos and cheerleading of fighters towards death has a flip side; the psychic, the care-giver, the kingmaker of her triple aspects show her complexity. They remind us that Morrígan's strength and drive in battle comes from her deep love for her country. She works to make sure the land is fertile, that the people are safe, that in death, they go safely to the next world. It is this passionate, tenacious nature that inspires her followers to find the strength to fight their own demons.

THE
VALKYRIES

NORSE: SPIRITS

Also known as
Valkyrja

Strong, beautiful, powerful, the Valkyries ride their horses bareback across the sky, shining with fierce femininity. Shield maidens of Odin, a leading Norse god, they carry the souls of the dead to eternal glory. However, their earlier incarnations were darker and more complex.

Norse warriors both dreaded and welcomed the thunderous hooves of the Valkyries' steeds. At the height of a bloody, noisy battle, the warrior maidens, dressed in shining armour and brandishing swords, would gallop between the clouds, swooping down and scooping up the bravest souls of those who perished by the sword and bearing the heroes to Odin's Valhalla, the hall of slain warriors. The Valkyries served meat and mead to Valhalla's heroes until they were called upon to fight in the final reckoning of Ragnarök, the battle in which all gods and men perish.

CHOOSERS OF THE SLAIN

Described in the thirteenth- and fourteenth-century Old Norse collection of sagas, the *Poetic Edda*, in their early incarnations the Valkyries were bloodthirsty, sometimes depicted as carrion-hunting ravens, with slavering pet wolves. Their name, 'Valkyries', literally means 'choosers of the slain' – they picked out the soldiers they would take, influencing the outcome of battles and using magic to direct the action. These rough, tough women were far from impartial – they protected or trained their favourite warriors, fell in love and acted upon grudges while meting out revenge on the battlefield. The northern lights were said to be the reflections of their shields and armour, and dew and hail would fall from their horses' manes.

One of the most lurid descriptions of the early Valkyries can be found in 'Helgakviða Hundingsbana I', a poem in the thirteenth-century Icelandic epic *Njáls saga*. This part of the story is set in Ireland, just before the Battle of Clontarf, a fight between Brian Boru, King of Ireland, and a Norse/Irish alliance. A man named Dörruð witnesses twelve Valkyries using a terrifying loom made from human remains. Severed heads serve as weights, a sword as the shuttle and its reels are made of arrows. The hideous tapestry is being woven using innards and guts for the warp and weft. The Valkyries gleefully spin the fortune of the armies, choosing who will die and working their fate into the flesh-cloth.

Later, their form became more romanticised – softer, blonder, more sentimental. They dropped the bone-looms and started to brush their hair and bronze their limbs. They were demoted to Odin's shield maidens, losing a little grit and idiosyncrasy as they slid into blander servitude – yet they remained strident, strong, willing to speak their minds.

The most famous Valkyrie was Brynhildr (Brunhild), whose complicated tale was told in the thirteenth-century *Völsunga saga*. Cursed by Odin, she was banished to a castle on top of a mountain to sleep until rescued by a man. Hero Sigurd entered the castle, fell in love with the blonde-haired shield maiden and cut off her armour. He then proposed, giving her a magic ring and left, promising to return and marry her. Brynhildr created a ring of fire around her castle and retreated, awaiting her love's return.

However, on his travels, Sigurd encountered an evil sorceress, Grimhild, who was determined the hero would marry her daughter, Gudrun. Grimhild drugged Sigurd with a magic potion, so that he forgot about his beloved Brynhildr and married Gudrun instead. To make sure there was no chance of reconciliation, Grimhild determined to marry Brynhildr off to her son, Gunnar. He, however, couldn't breach the flaming defences of Brynhildr's lair, so asked his brother-in-law, Sigurd, for help. Still under Grimhild's spell, Sigurd willingly swapped bodies with him, leaping over the fire. Brynhildr was impressed with this brave feat and the two shared a bed for three nights, although a combination of Grimhild's spell and Sigurd's innate nobility meant that nothing sexual took place. Gunnar and Sigurd swapped back and Brynhildr had no idea about the deception.

That was until Gudrun and Brynhildr argued about whose husband was the most brave. In the heat of the row, Gudrun revealed the duplicitous truth. Sigurd's memory suddenly returned, but although he tried to reason with Brynhildr, her fury swiftly turned into a desire for cold revenge on the lover whom she believed had spurned her. Totally without emotion, she urged her new husband, Gunnar, to kill Sigurd. He wouldn't, but his younger brother, Gutthorm, took on the challenge and murdered Sigurd in his sleep; the dying hero stabbed him mortally in return. Still Brynhildr raged; she 'flashed out fire, and ... snorted forth venom' and, in her fury, tragically killed Sigurd and Gunnard's three-year-old son before committing suicide by throwing herself onto Sigurd's funeral pyre.

> 'Now awful it is to be without, as blood-red rack races overhead; is the welkin gory with warriors' blood as we valkyries war-songs chanted.'
> – TRADITIONAL, DARRAÐARLJÓÐ

HERE COMES THE GANG

The Valkyries are possibly the only mythological beings who have their own memorable theme tune. Written as part of Wagner's *Ring Cycle*, the gloriously pompous, spine-tingling 'The Ride of the Valkyries' conjures up images of the maidens racing through the sky, high-fiving. It was used to dramatic effect in Francis Ford Coppola's 1979 film *Apocalypse Now*, set in the Vietnam War, where the brass-driven anthem blared out of speakers mounted onto helicopters as American soldiers senselessly attacked an innocent, peaceful village. The metal flying machines with their ear-shattering roar echo the mythical women, terrifying the villagers while flying gleefully over the chaotic, death-filled carnage below.

Norse mythology places much power in the hands of its female protagonists, and the Valkyries' ability to influence vital battles is impressive, placing them right at the heart of the action in many sagas. The Valkyries loved hard and fought harder. They were like a tough girl gang, only on horseback, with matching outfits, sharp blades, helmets and a 'live fast, die young' attitude. Their impact changed the course of history – they picked who would die or survive in some of Norse mythology's greatest battles – and has resounded down the centuries.

PONTIANAK

MALAY: GHOST

Also known as
Kuntilanak
Matianak
Kunti
Churel

Beware of a mysterious beautiful woman in a flowing white dress, her hair pulled over her face. She might just be a pontianak, a bad-tempered Malay·ghost with a particular taste for feeding on internal organs.

Although stories of these vampiric creatures are thought to have been around for millennia, solid documentation starts around the turn of the nineteenth century. Pontianak is a city on the west coast of Kalimantan (the Indonesian part of modern-day Borneo), said to have been named after the long-haired ghosts who haunted the region's first sultan, Syarif Abdurrahman Alkadrie (1730–1808). Some say he defeated the long-haired gut rippers, others that he was consumed by them. Still more tales of the fearsome female ghouls were documented by Western ethnographers when the area was colonised in the late nineteenth century.

The ghostly remnants of prehistoric animist beliefs, pontianaks are one of a pantheon of spooks found in South East Asia, swirled into Hindu and Buddhist traditions and absorbed into Muslim practices. Close relatives include Penanggalans, which manifest as the head of a woman trailing entrails, and the lang suir, banshees (see pages 126–29) that can transform into owls.

One school of thought believes the pontianaks are the spirits of women who have died in childbirth or while pregnant. Another that they are the ghosts of stillborn female children. Both forms manifest similarly and are out to get revenge for their own or their child's death.

By day, they live in banana trees, but come out at night, especially if there is a full moon in the sky. They may make their presence known by the bark of a dog or through baby cries that sound quieter as the spirit approaches. Or you might smell a pontianak before you see her, the scent of frangipani flowers drifting through the air. Her hair is long and pulled over her face. Scraped back it will reveal a beautiful, pale-skinned woman with red eyes, dressed in a blood-stained white dress, nails long and glinting in the moonlight. That sweet perfume will turn to the stink of rotting flesh as the woman's vulnerability turns to violent aggression and she transforms into her hideous, vampiric shape. Then she claws, ripping open her victim's stomach, pulling out the entrails and greedily sucking them down. Sometimes, she'll shred a man's genitals and, if she can, suck out his eyes. Pontianaks only attack men and there's only one way to stop them: by thrusting a coffin nail in the hole in the nape of their necks. This transforms them into subservient, docile, smiling wives – until that nail is removed.

FIGURES OF FEAR OR EMPOWERMENT

Pontianaks are still very much part of contemporary folklore, sightings reported in newspapers, uploaded online in murky, dark YouTube clips. Their white figures float along airless corridors in high-rise flats, across manicured communal parks, even in branches of Starbucks. Parents warn their children to behave or a pontianak will get them. They urge girls to be decorous and neat, so they don't look like, or behave like, one of the vampiric monsters.

This intense imagery was drawn on by schlocky film directors in the late 1950s, the release of a series of hugely popular pontianak films that ran until the early 1960s marked the birth of Malay horror as a genre. There's been a rekindling of the genre in the twentieth-century, as seen in the excellently named Malaysian film *Help Me, I'm a Pontianak* (2011). Kuala Lumpur-based filmmaker Amanda Nell Eu's short, *It's Easier*

'We live with a distinct double standard about male and female aggression. Women's aggression isn't considered real. It isn't dangerous; it's only cute. Or it's always self-defence or otherwise inspired by a man. In the rare case where a woman is seen as genuinely responsible, she is branded a monster – an "unnatural' woman".'

– KATHERINE DUNN

to Raise Cattle, turned the trope on its head, depicting a tender friendship between two girls, one of whom was a pontianak.

It's no coincidence that pontianaks surge in popularity each time society's sexual balance is threatened. Whether in the 1950s, when women started to assert their independence, or the 2000s, when the extreme Islamic fringes staked a claim on some of that autonomy, these figures could be seen to represent a fear of the power of women, a monsterising of those not conforming to the feminine 'norm' of raising a family. The vanquishing of these creatures in film equates to bringing those wild, boundary-transgressing women back under control. A nail in a pontianak's neck will tame the creature, turn her back into the 'ideal' woman, restore order, reinforce the patriarchy.

However, some contemporary Malaysian women have rejected the neutered pontianak, choosing to draw instead on the power and autonomy of the untamed creature. A pontianak can walk alone at night without fear. She represents the vengeance many cannot take on attackers, rapists and those who see females as inferior or who seek to inhibit their freedom. With her long, flesh-ripping nails and violent nature, the pontianak embodies these women's frustrations made corporeal. Perhaps her wild fury-filled lifestyle and rejection of conventional trappings appeal more than a life harnessed to the sink, the oven and the cradle.

BAOBHAN SITH

SCOTTISH: VAMPIRE

Beautiful yet ruthless, and with a taste for blood, the entrancing baobhan sith wreaks gory revenge on adulterers on behalf of her earthly sisters.

Across the world, there are tales of bands of female vampires – the succubi, Arabian qarînah and Jewish estries all take the form of beautiful women who seduce their victims (who are almost always men), either as they sleep or when they become tempted by the monsters' charms. A baobhan sith has an ethereal quality, part vampire, part ghost, part fairy and entirely terrifying.

A typical baobhan sith is usually found in the countryside, haunting forests, mountain paths and lonely, low roads. She favours green dresses – the preferred colour of fairies – worn long to conceal her hooved feet and can only stay out on the prowl until sunrise. Her breath hangs frostily in the air and she has powers to command the weather – dreich fogs and clouds the colour of otter fur disguise her movements and confuse travellers. She can shapeshift, appearing

as a wolf, crow or raven, but ultimately prefers the more seductive, earthy form of woman.

The baobhan sith are telepathic – they have no need for language. They also have a superhuman sense of smell, sniffing out hunters from the scent of blood on their clothes. These powers lead the sith to their prey, always male and often men who have wished for female company. They do have their kryptonite, however: they can't abide iron, while a stone placed on their grave will prevent them from rising.

The term 'sith' means 'people of the mounds', referring to those said to have occupied Scotland in prehistoric times. This suggests that the baobhan sith have been feared for millenia. However, they were at their most dreaded in the sixteenth to nineteenth centuries, when they were harnessed as propaganda against the heathens, the sound of women's hooves said to stamp and echo like the feet of the Devil.

One of the most famous stories of the baobhan sith concerns four hunters. They'd sheltered for the night in a remote bothy (small hut). A fire glowed in the hearth, they ate a good dinner and then the fun started – drinking and dancing. Although the night was merry, three of the men started discussing how it was a bit weird to have four guys dancing around on their own and how much better it might be if there were a few women around to liven things up. The fiddler disagreed and declared that he was happy with his wife and needed no company. Bang on cue, there was a knock at the door. When the men opened it, four beautiful women stood there, dressed in green. 'We are lost,' said one of the women. 'May we come inside and join you?'

At this point, you might think that the men would stop to consider what the chances were of a group of alluring women turning up in the middle of nowhere, asking to join the party. However, trousers (or kilts) ruled brains, even in ancient Scotland, and the ladies were invited in. The evening escalated; the guests paired off and the dance became wilder.

However, the musician noticed something disturbing, drops of blood dripping from one of the women. He looked more closely and as she danced, she raised the hem of her dress, her hooves peeping beneath. The women, realising their secret was out, drew out their long nails, slashing at the necks of their dance partners. Terrified, the musician threw down his fiddle and raced out into the cold night. The woman he'd been speaking to chased him, her long talons scraping at the back of his neck, but he managed to outrun her and hid among the horses. Although she tried to get nearer to him, something prevented her from getting close – the iron horseshoes were protecting him.

Realising all he could do was stay put, the man spent a long, cold night with the horses. As dawn broke, he wandered back to the house in a daze. On opening the door, he was confronted with the sight of his dead friends, drained of blood, their bodies desiccated on the floor.

This story of the baobhan sith acted as a cautionary tale, nudging men to stay faithful to their wives. It's also thought that the saga of the hunters may have emerged at a time when dancing was frowned upon by the Christian Church, the tale being a tool to keep folk respectfully sober. The sith's sexuality, their carefree behaviour represent everything the Church at the time feared.

THE SITH IN MODERN CULTURE

The baobhan sith and female vampire trope have fed into countless books and films, from Dracula's coterie to lurid lesbian bloodsucker movies – even Darth Vader's forces share their name. More recently, you can feel the sith's vibrations in films such as *Under The Skin*, based on Michel Faber's book of the same name, in which an alien Scarlett Johansson bleakly wanders a modern Scotland, seducing men with brutal, cold efficiency and condemning them to a life submerged in black goo.

The baobhan sith could be seen to be similarly chilly; their only function to seduce men. But their rejection of the traditional female role makes them interesting. The violence is calculated, but, like the Furies (pages 64–67), they pick their victims for a reason: their infidelity, their transgressions – the sith are vigilantes acting on behalf of those women left at home while their husbands hunt, dance, flirt. They are socially subversive, turning gender constructs on their head, destroyers rather than creators. They are not afraid to use violence in order to further an important social agenda.

Essentially, if you are worried your travelling partner is thinking of straying, rest easy – the baobhan sith have your back.

LILITH

Also known as
Lilit
Lilitu
Lillu
Lilin

In Jewish myth, the first woman wasn't the subservient Eve, it was radical feminist Lilith. Now, after centuries of being demonised for her sexually confident attitude, she is taking on a new role as a girl-positive folk heroine.

Lilith first appears in Sumerian epic poem Gilgamesh and the Huluppu-Tree (2000 BCE) as a demoness banished by Gilgamesh. A terracotta plaque from the same era depicts her naked with bird wings, horns and taloned feet. She was believed to steal Babylonian children and was only warded off by amulets and charms – tales of her exploits spread across the region.

By the time the Bible was written, Lilith seems to have become a byword for night demons across the near East. In the book of Isaiah, her one mention in the Bible, she is described as living in desolate places and is compared to a 'screech owl'. Perhaps this is because of her nocturnal activities, but it also places her in the pantheon of mythological women and goddesses associated with the bird, such as Athena (Greek), Blodeuwedd (Celtic), Lakshmi (Hindu), Hi'iaka

(Hawaiian), the lang suir (Malaysian, see the Pontianak, pages 98–101) and La Diablesse (Caribbean). In the Talmud, the compilation of Jewish religious law written c. 500–600 CE, a demonic Lilith was described as having long hair and wings and portrayed as a vampiric succubus who would visit men at night, bring them to climax as they slept and steal their sperm to inseminate herself and create legions of illegitimate demon children. As a result, men were warned to never sleep alone in the house. This incarnation served both as a warning against the salacious side of the night – wild sensuality, freedom – and to dissuade young men from masturbation, regarded by the Jewish rabbis as a deadly sin.

Lilith's role as Adam's wife was first codified in the *Alphabet of Ben Sira*. This was a medieval midrash – an almost satirical interpretation of the events documented in the *Bible* with a sprinkling of oral folklore from the Jewish tradition – from sometime between 700 and 1000 CE. These writings muse on two contrasting accounts of Adam's first wife in Genesis, concluding that the self-confident Lilith was moulded from the same clay at the same time as Adam and that she was his equal in the Garden of Eden. Immediately after her creation by God, Lilith questioned Adam about the presumed order of things, a conversation that erupted into a fruity argument about sex. Adam told her that he expected things to happen missionary style, with her underneath, inferring that he would also be in the driving seat in the relationship. Lilith laughed in his face, 'You lie beneath me. We are both equal, for both of us are from the earth.' The argument escalated, ending with Lilith using God's name in anger and flying off into the night. A furious Adam prayed to God for help and God ordered three of his angels, Senoy, Sansenoy and Semangelof, to give chase. God also had a one-to-one with the distraught Adam, saying threateningly, 'If she wants to return, all the better. If not, she will have to accept that one hundred of her children (demons) will die every day.'

'You lie beneath me. We are both equal, for both of us are from the earth.'

The angels tracked down Lilith to her hideout next to the Red Sea and explained God's terms. So Lilith made her choice. She picked loneliness and the loss of her demonic children over subservience: she refused to return. God's punishment came to pass and each day a hundred of her offspring were slain. But her threats were not hollow and she wreaked her revenge on human children: 'I was created only to cause sickness to infants. If the infant is male, I have dominion over him for eight days after his birth, and if female, for twenty days.'

And so Lilith became a folkloric baby-killing demon, the winged cause of stillbirths and cot deaths, although she did make one concession to her pursuers – that newborns wearing an amulet with the three angels' names or images would be spared. She was too much for Adam. He, of course, went on to marry a meeker wife, Eve, created from his rib.

Lilith was literally and figuratively demonised. It has been suggested that, as is often the case with besmirched goddesses, her banishment represented a warning to women who might be minded to demand more rights. Eve was held up as (almost) everything a contemporaneous Jewish woman should have been: subservient, enabling, her only vice being a taste for the forbidden fruit of sex. Lilith, on the other hand, representsed freedom, the shaking off of the shackles of marriage, impulsivity and certainty in one's beliefs. These two women, one beta, one alpha, could be the two halves of every woman – one who fulfils everything that is expected of her by society, the other who is more reckless and refuses to conform.

By the time the *Kabbalic Zohar* was written, in twelfth-century Spain, Lilith was depicted not just as Adam's first wife, but as the consort of Satan, a night-flying temptress in the same mould as her *Talmud* incarnation, and the chaotic yang to the Shekhinah (the divine feminine side of God's ying). And it's this dark take on Lilith that really pervades the Jewish folkloric tradition across the near East and Europe. This association with all-consuming evil made her a dark muse for artists: Michelangelo portrayed her as half-woman, half-serpent; poet Dante Gabriel Rossetti described her fair hair as 'The first gold'; and writer James Joyce called her the 'patron of abortions' in his seminal *Ulysses*. C.S. Lewis' White Witch is described in *The Lion, The Witch and The Wardrobe* by Mr Beaver as coming from 'your father Adam's ... first wife, her they called Lilith'.

RECLAIMING LILITH

In more recent times, Lilith has been rebranded. *The Coming of Lilith*, a 1972 story by Judith Plaskow Goldenberg, sees the exiled wife returning to Eden and bonding with Eve, a friendship and alliance that disturbs both Adam and God. This multi-dimensional Lilith was the woman who became a second-wave feminist icon, lending her name to a female-centric, Jewish culture magazine and the late 1990s' all-woman travelling music festival, Lilith Fair. Lilith's story is further explored and gently echoed in the award-winning TV drama *Killing Eve* (2018), the 'good' and 'evil' female lead characters locked in mutual obsession to the horror of their male companions.

It's appropriate that Lilith's name is finally being reclaimed. That the first woman in the Jewish world was an unapologetic feminist is positive. Her defiance and refusal to be a submissive wife may have resulted in a millennia-long exile in the wilderness, yet her long overdue rehabilitation is a cause for celebration.

LOVIATAR

FINNISH: GODDESS

Also known as
Loveatar
Lovetar
Lovehetar
Louhetar
Louhiatar
Louhi

She's evil, short-tempered and hideously ugly – and her nine children wreaked havoc across the world in the form of fatal diseases and ailments. Loviatar is the Finnish goddess we love to hate.

Loviatar was the daughter of Tuoni and Tuonetar, the king and queen of the Underworld. Her parents were renowned for their grim hospitality; Tuonetar's signature cocktail was 'The Beer of Oblivion', a poison made of frogspawn, poisonous snakes, lizards and worms, which caused everyone who sipped it to forget their very existence.

Loviatar was considered to have the blackest heart of the couple's children, no mean feat as they included Kalma, goddess of death and decay, and Kipu-Tyttö, goddess of illness. She was described in the nineteenth-century poem 'The Kalevala' by Finnish-born writer Elias Lönnrot in unequivocal terms, as the 'Evil genius of Lappala'.

Although a virgin, she was impregnated by Iku-Turso, the wind. Loviatar carried her heavy unborn children for nine years, all the while miserable and

in constant pain. Her labour was horrific; she spent it in agony, writhing around streams, whirlpools and volcanoes, across the tundra and wandering through the chilling winds. According to 'The Kalevala', she found her way to the 'never pleasant' north, where she was met by wicked Queen Louhi who invited her into her halls and acted as her midwife. The queen poured her a beer and showed her to the sauna, where she helped the goddess give birth to her nine sons.

WREAKING HAVOC

Loviatar named eight of the boys Consumption, Colic, Gout, Rickets, Ulcer, Scab, Cancer and Plague and they represented 'All the ills and plagues of Northland'. Her last son was the nameless human representative of perhaps the most awful plague of all, Envy. In some stories, she also gave birth to a girl, whom she killed immediately. The nine siblings of destruction were sent to the city of Kalevala to wreak havoc, but were thwarted by Väinämöinen, a heroic sage who healed his people with saunas and an encyclopaedic knowledge of herbal remedies. Of course, although he won the battle, the disease-golems won the war and eventually succeeded in their quest for global domination.

Although in Lönnrot's nineteenth-century telling, Loviatar is helped by a separate Louhi, in older folk tales, the two names are used interchangeably. Louhi seems to represent a more positive alter-ego of the goddess, one with the power to shape shift and wield powerful magic. In early stories, she was a moon goddess, connected to the dead through the stars and the northern lights. However, by the time 'The Kalevala' was written, in 1848, she had diverged fully from Loviatar and become demonised, the embodiment of the pagan faith, vanquished by the wizard Väinämöinen, who represented the new Christian religion.

THE TRUE SURVIVOR

Loviatar has survived in fragments down the ages. Even into the nineteenth century, she was invoked in charms during childbirth. She has, unsurprisingly, found fans in popular culture, in the video-gaming and modern doom-metal community, where bands are named after her, while Icelandic punk bands write songs in her honour.

> 'Black in heart, and soul, and visage, Evil genius of Lappala, Made her couch along the wayside, On the fields of sin and sorrow.'
> – TRADITIONAL, 'THE KALEVALA'

It might seem hard to find anything positive to say about this goddess who ruled over death and disease, who gave birth to such evil, who even possibly committed the ultimate transgression of killing her own child, a girl. She has no redeeming graces: she's grumpy, sullen and her only relationship seems to be with someone equally troubled, Louhi. But every pantheon of stories needs a cartoon villain, someone to rail against, for heroes to vanquish – without them, there is no story, no grit, no resolution. Loviatar teaches us what can happen if a deity chooses evil over good.

Even this most evil of goddesses, however, did not succeed in her mission to destroy humankind. She threw everything she had, the nine most evil children-plague hybrids, at us, yet we remain, we survive. And in this, the failure of her nine plagued children to wreak utter destruction on our planet, Loviator might also be seen as a warped emblem of humankind's sheer resilience.

HARPIES

The name of these terrifying, scavenging monsters – the half-bird, half-human embodiment of the storm winds became a byword for nagging, 'shrill' women. But the term is now close to standing for any woman who demands change.

The harpies, Aello (Storm Swift) and Ocypete (Swift Wing) were first described by Hesiod in around 700 BCE as beautiful winged maidens personifying the storm winds. By the time they were mentioned by the playwright Aeschylus in the fourth or fifth century BCE, they had been transformed into monsters, with metal talons and vulture-like wings, tails and legs. Their faces were still those of women, but they were haggard with hunger; despite scavenging food like carrion birds, they were always ravenous. They made a habit of defecating everywhere and smelled rank. They represented everything a Greek woman shouldn't be – greedy, ugly, loud, unhygenic. The original pair, Aello and Ocypete, were now three or more and, as they became more monstrous, the harpies' numbers grew.

Zeus, Hera and Athena used the repulsive gang as gunslingers for hire and would send them to punish those who had fallen from grace.

The insatiable monsters also played a role in the tale of Jason and the Argonauts. During their quest, the fleece chasers washed up on a remote island where they found blind King Phineas. He had been given the gift of fortune-telling, but had angered Zeus by having visions that revealed the gods' secret schemes. To punish the king, Zeus took away his sight and banished him to the island, but his final torture was worthy of a Bond villain. Every day, Zeus laid on a lavish buffet and, as starving Phineas went to help himself, a gang of harpies would descend, stealing the food, before gleefully defecating on the table.

An appalled Jason pledged to help poor, hungry Phineas, and he enlisted the brute strength of the Boreads, the sons of the Boreas, the god of north wind. Together, the wind brothers drove away the harpies, chasing them ceaselessly across the world, until their sister, the goddess Iris intervened and the half-women, half-birds escaped to a cave on Crete. A grateful Phineus told Jason how to navigate the tricky Symplegades rocks, which crashed together each time a vessel passed through.

Human disappearances were also blamed on these super-swift monsters – even noble women were vulnerable, the bounty-hunting harpies flying off with the daughters of King Pandareos, stealing them from their foster mother Aphrodite and taking them to act as servants for the goddesses of vengeance, the Furies (see pages 64–67). The harpies could also go rogue, stealing meals, destroying houses and crops and whipping up storms, seemingly on a whim. The ancient Greeks blamed them when food or valuable items went missing or for sudden disasters.

The shrieking, hungry beasts are part of the pantheon of beings worldwide whose task it is to bear away the souls of the dead, like Morrígan (pages 90–93) and the Valkyries (pages 94–97). It's a strong archetype and, through literature and art, these vividly portrayed creatures live on. Their distinctive shape appears on temple carvings and vases, while Roman and Byzantine writers kept their name alive. In the Middle Ages, they pop up in the seventh ring of Hell in Dante's *Inferno*, infesting a haunted wood where the bodies of those who had committed suicide were absorbed into the trees. This scene was immortalised by William Blake in his 1824–27 painting *The Wood of the Self-Murderers*.

Thanks to their eye-catching role in the *Golden Fleece* saga, the harpies also make cameo appearances in adaptations of the story, including, memorably, in Ray Harryhausen's 1963 film *Jason and the Argonauts* – their screeching, whirlwind appearance sending generations of TV-watching kids scuttling behind their sofas.

However, these monstrous entities' name has also been appropriated for something perhaps more terrifying than their original incarnation. Benedick, in Shakespeare's *Much Ado About Nothing*, says of forthright

'I raise up my voice – not so I can shout, but so that those without a voice can be heard . . . we cannot succeed when half of us are held back.'

– MALALA YOUSAFZAI

Beatrice that he would rather do hard labour than 'hold three words conference with this harpy!' The term 'harpy' has crystallised into an intensely gendered byword for any woman too demanding, too loud, taking up too much room or audio space. It suggests shrew, scold, dragon, battle-axe, banshee – or, increasingly, feminist.

It dogged Victorian women as they made their move from the domestic to the professional arena. Even as ladies made their first tentative steps into politics, it was whispered behind their backs in the corridors of power. In 1872, the first woman to run for president of the United States, Victoria Woodhull, was called a 'harpy'. And those whispers soon became shouts. A Google search for 'Hillary Clinton' and 'harpy' will throw up over 60,000 results. The term defined men's boundaries: you may take what we give you from the table, but woe betide you should help yourself.

WE ARE HARPIES

The word 'harpy' is now tossed at any woman who steps outside what are considered society's 'norms'. Women who are regarded as too ambitious, too loud, too demanding. Those who are angry and fighting for social change. Women who are too sexy. Women who aren't sexy enough. In discourse online and off, it's a way of shutting down questions and debate, of reducing someone to a stereotype, an easy path out of rational argument, ranking alongside 'snowflake', 'libtard' or 'whining millennial'.

Now is the time to reclaim the term 'harpy', to de-weaponise it, to harness it in a positive fashion or, at the very least, to question and pull up those who seek to use it as a term of abuse. In order to be accepted in a more polarised world, our heroines must become more obscene, casting aside what is polite, civilised, acceptable, in order to swoop down and grab what is rightfully theirs.

We will not wait to be offered the leftovers from the feast. We will arrive in a whirl of wings and talons and pick off what belongs to us. Yes, we are angry, yes we are making a noise about it, and yes, we are hungry for change. We are harpies.

MEDUSA

GREEK/ROMAN: MONSTER

Grisly in appearance, her Gorgon head ringed in writhing serpents, with a face that transformed anyone gazing directly upon it into stone, Medusa's hideous looks were double-edged, both her curse and her super power. Although her dramatic appearance may still entrance and repel, today, she's been reclaimed as a poster girl for strong, outspoken women and survivors of traumatic events.

The three Gorgon sisters were born to sea gods Phorcys and Ceto. According to the poet Hesiod, while Sthenno and Euryale were immortal, the beautiful, golden-haired Medusa was human. In Ovid's telling, Medusa's fair locks caught the attention of sea god Poseidon, who callously raped her in a temple dedicated to the goddess Athena (Minerva in Roman versions). Furious at this desecration, Athena committed the ultimate victim-blame, cursing Medusa with reptilian tresses and a grotesque face.

Now regarded as so monstrous that even a glimpse of her countenance would result in the onlooker

being rendered immovable, Medusa transformed into a super-villain. And so powerful was Athena's spell, that Medusa's siblings, Sthenno and Euryale, were also turned into monsters with dragon-like scales, huge wings and sharp fangs and claws. The fiercely loyal sisters retreated to a cave on the island of Sarpedon.

THE STONIEST GAZE

We know very little of Medusa's personal story for the next few years, her life or internal dialogue – anything bar her transformation and its effect on her visitors. Was she cowed by her appearance? Hurt and hardened into imperious revenge by Athena's betrayal? Or empowered by her new gift of petrification? It's rather wonderful to imagine that she regarded herself as still attractive and that, as French feminist theorist Hélène Cixous suggested in her essay, 'The Laugh of the Medusa', if you had the courage to look her in the eye: 'she's not deadly. She's beautiful and laughing.'

After a career in solidifying any warrior who dared enter her cave, Medusa encountered demi-god Perseus who had been tricked by his foe, Polydectes, into accepting a quest to capture the head of the Gorgon. He enlisted help from Hermes and Athena, and travelled to the lair of the three Graiae, who were also sisters to the Gorgons. The Graiae possessed one tooth and one eye between them, both of which Perseus seized and refused to give back until they spilled the beans on Medusa's whereabouts. Armed with enchanted objects to aid him in his adventure, Perseus found his way to Medusa's cave. There he used his polished shield as a mirror to sneak up on a sleeping Medusa, thus allowing him to look at her reflection rather than her actual face so avoiding petrification. He killed Medusa with one stroke of his sword, decapitating her, before taking her head and putting it in a bag. As the blood drained from her body, two drops hit the ground, turning immediately into fabulous animal figures, Pegasus, the winged horse, and Chrysler, a winged boar – both the offspring of Poseidon, the god who had raped her all those years before. Medusa's sisters pursued Perseus, determined to avenge her death, but, using his cap of invisibility, he evaded them.

'I thought Medusa had looked at you and that you were turning to stone. Perhaps now you will ask how much you are worth?'
- CHARLOTTE BRONTË, *JANE EYRE*

Even in her cadaverous state, Medusa had a death stare that had lost none of its potency and Perseus used her head as a kind of totemic weapon, hauling it from his sack and dangling it in front of his enemies, thus turning them into stone. It eventually ended up in the possession of Athena, who set it on her shield to ward off evil. This is perhaps the ultimate humiliation – Athena, the woman who turned Medusa into a monster, using her enemy's dead face to assert and bolster her own power.

The Medusa myth has fascinated and entranced many, reverberating through popular culture. Her visage has been used as a protective charm, set into buildings and famously emblazoned on Alexander the Great's shield. She's been immortalised in paintings by Caravaggio, Rubens and Leonardo da Vinci, sculptures by Cellini, Canova and Dalí and fleshed out in literature by Shelley and Iris Murdoch. Even today, her (premonsterised) face shines from Versace's logo.

More politically, Medusa has become shorthand for a particular brand of strong female agency perceived as aggressive or 'unladylike'. Marie Antoinette was depicted with snake-like hair in French seventeenth-century cartoons, while in the early twentieth century, anti-suffragette postcards likened the protesters to the monster. During the 2016 American election campaign, the image of Hillary Clinton's snake-bedecked, raging head being cut off by her Republican rival Donald Trump – compared to Perseus – appeared on unofficial merchandise. Similarly, another strong female leader, German chancellor Angela Merkel, has found herself depicted as a Gorgon. These portrayals reinforce a millennia-old message from men to women: keep your mouth shut or we'll shut it for you. It seems that if a woman has a point of view and a voice, an online troll's hand will be hovering over their mouse, ready to Photoshop snakes onto that woman's head. Classicist Mary Beard wrote, depressingly, in *Women & Power: A Manifesto* (2017): 'There have been all kinds of well-known feminist attempts over the last fifty years or more to reclaim Medusa for female power ... but it's made not a blind bit of difference to the way she has been used in attacks on female politicians.'

Medusa now embodies the monsterising and silencing through violence of modern women who dare to speak out, get angry or put their heads above the parapet. She survived a vicious rape, for which she was blamed and cursed – something that directly presages the twenty-first century global #MeToo movement riling against sexual abuse, violence and harassment.

Alluring and multifaceted, the figure of Medusa remains an enigma employed variously as a symbol of fury, protection, agency, victimhood or strength. In her cursed state, Medusa gains power, the power to kill with her looks, to turn to stone. She's derided as hideous, yet still fascinates. There is a duality, a mystery to her. Even in death, even when silenced, the strength embodied in Medusa's looks is both feared and revered.

LA LLORONA

Deeply embedded in Mexican culture and folklore, La Llorona, 'the weeping woman' is the spirit of a woman who has transgressed one of society's ultimate taboos – infanticide.

Mesmerisingly beautiful, La Llorona is said to stalk the banks of the Rio Grande and bodies of water across Mexico and the wider diaspora, clad in a tattered, white dress, her long black hair shining like moonlit water. She keens and wails into the night '*Ay, mis hijos!*' ('Oh, my children') and floats inches above the shallows. Even in contemporary Mexico and across the southern states of America, sightings are reported, and youngsters still warned not to wander too close to the river at night, '... or La Llorona will get you!' If she spots an errant child, she will haul her screaming and terrified into the deeper water, holding her under until her little body becomes lifeless.

Each Mexican town or village has its own story of this child-killing spirit. However, the most popular has it that Maria, as La Llorona was known when she was human, was a sparky, beautiful peasant girl who caught the eye of a playboy nobleman. The pair fell in love and the man put his carousing ways behind him. Making a home in Maria's village, they had two sons. Maria was a devoted mother, but her husband didn't appreciate her work; he returned to his old ways, drinking, staying out late and philandering. One day, as Maria walked by the river late at night, a carriage drove by, carrying her husband who was kissing another woman. Maria exploded with rage, ran back to the house and pulled her sons from their beds. She took them to the river and drowned them, then let the waters close above her head to share their fate. On reaching the gates of heaven, she was told that the souls of her boys were missing, so she returned to earth, condemned to search for her children into eternity. To this day, she searches. Some say that she also takes men who are drunk or cheating on their wives.

WATER, WATER EVERYWHERE

Historically, La Llorona's ongoing presence served as a cautionary tale to teenage girls to stay away from fast-living boys, but also to keep children wary of open bodies of water. This fear was vital at a time before running water was common in homes and even very small children were sent to collect it for household use. Drowning was, and still is, a common cause of death in pre-teens worldwide, and using stories of terrifying bogeywomen was an effective, pre-television and pre-digital-age method of instilling a healthy respect for the dangers of water.

There are similar tales of child-grabbing beasts and hungry spirits lurking in open bodies of water from other parts of the globe: the duckweed-garlanded Jenny Greenteeth from the north of England and her gloriously named watery sisters across the UK, Nellie Longarms, Peg Powler and the river hag Ginny Burntarse; the Slavic rusalka, Japanese kappa and hulking bunyips of Australia. Although the tale of Maria has been documented for over four centuries, some believe there are elements of a more ancient mystic DNA in the tale, the Aztec goddess Cihuacōātl or 'Snake Woman', for example, wore white and stalked dark nights, weeping, while children were sacrificed to water goddess Coatlicue.

Another theory is that Maria's story sprang from that of La Malinche, the indigenous woman who served as translator for the fifteenth-century Spanish conquistador Hernán Cortés. She became Cortés' mistress, bearing him a child, but he cast her aside for a Spanish woman. Seen by her own people as a traitor, La Malinche, according to popular lore, killed her son in an act of bloody vengeance – although there appears to be no historical evidence for this. This version of La Llorona's tale is a wider metaphor for the loss of indigenous culture after the country was invaded by the Spanish.

La Llorona's tale is fluid enough to reflect the concerns of each generation – for the conquered peoples, it represents their loss of identity and history. More recently, she has been viewed as a feminist icon. Stephanie Surrano writes in *No More Tears: La Llorona at the Crossroads of Feminism* (2011): 'The newer adaptations of the story illustrate an evolving, changing Chicana and, more specifically, dynamic perspectives of Chicana motherhood ... exploding the myth of mother as either passive and weak or loving and nurturing.'

Those adaptations include, unsurprisingly, horror films – La Llorona has been a stalwart B-movie character since the 1960s and appears in TV shows and video games. It's hard not to see her as the inspiration behind The Bride in Tarantino's cult film *Kill Bill* – the thin, shuffling, dust-billowing, ghostly figure coming out of the dark, a character who believes she is responsible for the death of her child.

'La Llorona makes corporeal the fears of many women struggling with motherhood: the deep well of postnatal emotion that can easily be suffocating as well as joyous.'

Further back, a version of Llorona's tale has floated into the ears of Mexicans for decades, if not centuries. The folk song 'La Llorona' soundtracks Day of the Dead festivities. Its lyrics are told from the point of view of a man whose lover cries each time he tries to leave her, and there are well-known versions by musicians such as Raphael, Eugenia León and Joan Baez. You'll hear it in the background of films such as *Frida* (2002) and *Coco* (2017).

La Llorona makes corporeal the fears of many women struggling with motherhood; the deep well of postnatal emotion that can be as easily suffocatingly dark as joyous. The paranoia of losing your identity or that your partner's emotions may not be in step with yours. She embodies the fear of rejection even the most assertive of new mothers suffer: if they focus too much on their children, will their partner become resentful?

In a twisted way, La Llorona could be seen to give these women strength, a voice, an indication that they're not alone in having these powerful, terrifying feelings. A spark of solidarity, of sisterhood, in the long, hormone-fugged night.

BANSHEE

Also known as
Bean sí
Baintsí
Ben síde
Baintsíde

The siren wail of the banshee piercing the night is chilling. Not just its quavering pitch, harsh and eerie, but also because of what the shriek represents, the imminent death of a family member – loss and devastation. But is the fear of the banshee's moan rooted more deeply in the elemental power of the female voice?

Although you'll recognise a banshee or *bean-sídhe* (literally, 'fairy-woman') by her high-pitched scream, her appearance varies. She might appear as a beautiful young woman wearing a silver dress, with glittering white or shimmering red hair flowing down her back. Alternatively, she'll look like an old crone caked in dirt with long fingernails and rotten teeth, or perhaps as a headless lady carrying a bowl of blood, naked from the waist up. These different looks echo the triple aspect of the goddess Morrígan (see pages 90–93), on whom many believe the shrieking spirits are based. Many of the death-screamers have red eyes, rubbed raw from centuries of tears and they often carry a silver comb – even today, many Irish people are reluctant to pick

127

up a discarded comb for fear of angering a fairy. Despite her sometimes gruesome appearance, a banshee is usually fairly benign. She might cry outside a house during the nights preceding a demise or appear to a family member. Some claim that the ancient Celtic noble families each have their own and a family banshee was seen as a status symbol. When families emigrated, they would sometimes take their banshee along with them to the New World, but often the ghost would be left behind, mourning the loss of its charges.

> 'I'm in a wild mood tonight. I want to go dance in the foam. I hear the banshees calling.'
> – RAYMOND CHANDLER,
> *FAREWELL MY LOVELY*

A banshee even foretold the death of kings: in 1437, King James I of Scotland was said to have been approached by an Irish diviner – a banshee in human form – who foretold his murder in a plot hatched by the Earl of Atholl. He took no notice.

Some believe that the banshee had her origins in the harsh, strange calls of owls (see also the Pontianak, pages 98–101), describing how a banshee's skirts made the sound of over-sized, beating wings, and the way she flew through the air like a giant bird.

Banshees have mythological ancestors, the similarly bird-like Greek harpies (see pages 114–117). They also have cousins. In Scotland, contemporaneous with the banshees was the duck-footed, one-toothed, droopy-breasted bean-nighe, or 'washer woman'. She could be found singing a lament as she washed bloody shrouds in a loch or ford – a tale perhaps stitched from the remnants of the story of Morrígan (see pages 90–93).

Banshees were first mentioned in print by Seán Mac Craith in the fourteenth-century historical account *Cathreim Thoirdhealbhaigh*. One of his creatures says, 'I am "the Water-doleful", that in this land's hill-dwellings often sojourn, but in my origin I am of Hell's tuatha; and to invite you all I am come now, for but a little while and you and I shall be denizens of one country.' In common with the Irish goddess/fairy race Tuatha Dé Danann (see Morrígan and Brigid, pages 186–89) the banshees were thought to live in the Iron Age burial mounds that dot Ireland's meadows. Their mournful klaxon-like intonation accompanied soldiers into that unknown land, death.

It's this grief-filled wail, known mortally as the practice of keening, that was said to have been invented by the goddess Brigid, who shrieked over her son's broken body. It's believed that the banshees' corporeal manifestations were the eighth-century women who were paid in alcohol to mourn someone's passing and ease their passage to the Other World by singing sad laments or crying at the graveside, 'keeners'. Catholic women would continue to 'keen' until the twentieth century, despite the practice being frowned upon by the Church. It's a tradition that still happens in other parts of the world, but in Ireland's recent history has been stifled. It's almost as if the Church feared this manifestation of grief, that the sounds of despair were too raw, too primitive, too emotional. Replaced with a stiff upper lip, women's emotions and voices were silenced. The priests took back responsibillity for funerals, their neat order of service scripted by the male-dominated Church, and any random, purging and loud grief contained.

I AM BANSHEE, HEAR ME SCREAM

In contemporary culture, there are two types of banshee. One is the traditional, protective, kindly spirit who has a deep connection to her allotted family and whose song mourns impending loss. The other, modern incarnation, is more hateful, ugly. Her bloodied screams celebrate coming death and she is even said to hound her victims to an early grave with her screeches. You'll find her in video games, horror films and even in episodes of the popular cartoon *Scooby Doo*.

This reductive archetype has been used to damaging effect. In an online 2018 rant, Courtland Sykes, a US Republican Party candidate, described working mothers as 'career-obsessed banshees'. This comparison draws on an old trope – that women and, in particular, women's voices, are hen-pecking, high-pitched, annoying. Throughout her political life, Hillary Clinton has been ridiculed for her 'cackle', her 'shrill' voice. She is an example of gender congruence bias; that if a woman doesn't behave in a way deemed appropriate by society, people will not 'like' her and vote for her. There is evidence that women globally have deepened their voices in order to be taken more seriously in the workplace, and that women who consistently talk in deeper tones earn more.

This discomfort with women's natural voices is evident in the world of music, too. Female singers are expected to have pretty voices yet men can have 'character'. Punk rock movement women confounded this expectation – Siouxsie Sioux named her band after the creatures – but the influence runs deeper. X-Ray Spex's 'Oh Bondage, Up Yours!' begins with a solemn incantation from lead singer Poly Styrene, but ends in her screaming out the title. This rejection of the standard voice was used by other women who wanted to disrupt the musical status quo (and Status Quo): Big Mama Thornton's guttural growl, the gritty bark of Janis Joplin, Courtney Love's cathartic yell, Tina Turner's shriek in 'River Deep, Mountain High', Huggy Bear's radical screams, Kesha's whistle-howl in 'Praying', Bjørk's keens and screeches which shock and jolt her audience out of complacency. These raw, jagged voices echo the banshee, demanding to be listened to, inspiring future generations to throw their heads back and wail.

FUTAKUCHI-ONNA

Historically, many societies required women to dampen down their thoughts, to remain quiet, to eat decorously and to conform to accepted societal norms. Meet the futakuchi-onna, the twin-mouthed monsters who represent the logical conclusion of following those rules; that the consequences of that repression must manifest somewhere.

Futakuchi-onna are one of many thousands of Japanese *yōkai* – a pantheon of ghost monsters. Part of the country's culture since at least the first century CE, you'll see these spirits on ancient scrolls and prints and read about them in historical texts. However, it was after a collection of their stories was anthologised in Sekien Toriyama's 1776 *Gazu Hyakki Yako* that *yōkai* became a fad. Interest in *yōkai* was rekindled by fin-de-siècle journalist Lafcadio Hearn who anthologised Japanese legends that inspired the country's people to rediscover their traditional folklore.

Yōkai stalk the countryside and lurk on urban streets and, while they may have been around for millennia, they feel fiercely modern. Masters of adaptation, they metamorphosise and reflect the superstitions and worries of the times in which they exist. Their stories could fill a book alone, Jorōgumo, a shape-shifting spider woman, Teke Teke, a vengeful spirit of a girl cut in half by a train, Aka Manto, a malicious ghost who haunts toilets, asking if you want red or blue paper – red signalling that you will be sliced apart, blue that your blood will be sucked from your body.

However, the futakuchi-onna represent more than pure horror. At first, and even second, glance, a typical manifestation will resemble a conventional woman, her (somewhat strange) defining characteristic is a small appetite. However, her long, dark hair hides a gruesome secret – at the back of her head she has a huge, gaping mouth, hungry for food which she shovels in with tendrils of hair that act like grasping tentacles. In addition, the mouth mutters abuse, a sweary running commentary.

ORIGINS

Futakuchi-onna are thought to originate as humans, however a curse or disease transforms them into supernatural creatures. They star in many stories and one of the best known concerns a miserly man. He refused to marry or start a family due to the potential food bills. So when he met a woman with a bird-like appetite, he was overjoyed and proposed almost immediately. His new wife was a hard worker and seemed barely to eat, which pleased his thrifty nature, and yet he was confused by the speed at which his stocks of food were disappearing. One day, he stayed at home to spy on his wife and was horrified to see her kneeling on the floor, her hair cramming rice balls into her second, maw-like mouth. In some tales, she has been sent to teach the miser a lesson, in others the mouth has self-manifested, spawned from the woman's voluntary parsimony and sense of self-denial.

Another tale describes how futakuchi-onna were sometimes formed as a punishment. A human woman had indulged her own offspring with food and drink while neglecting her step-child, who died of starvation. Forty-nine days later (the traditional time for mourning in Japan), her husband accidentally struck the back of her head with his axe. The wound refused to heal; lips formed at its edges, teeth started to sprout and a tongue grew. As well as demanding food, the mouth constantly berated the woman for her transgression.

Yokai have been mined for inspiration by pop culture for decades, the dramatic, graphic futakuchi-onna make for arresting manga storylines, video game characters and horror film and TV villains. Appropriately, for a phenomenon that once rivalled the remarkably similar Pokémon, futakuchi-onna inspired one of the game's collectable creatures – Mawile, even her name echoes that of a gaping orifice.

The parallels with real women's lives sing out in the tale of the futakuchi-onna. She's an almost cartoon-like representation of the spectrum of eating disorders; a woman who denies herself food during the day in order to seem 'respectable' or conform to society's expectations, only to over-compensate with night-time binges. Her second mouth can be seen as a literal manifestation of a woman's suppression of her natural need for nourishment.

> 'If a woman eats she may destroy her spell, and if she will not eat, she destroys our dinner.'
> –BENJAMIN DISRAELI

The swearing and unpleasant rhetoric that emerge from her second hidden orifice embodies another form of suppression – being silenced. Historically Japanese women (and women worldwide) were warned that speaking out and having an opinion are not only unattractive to men but not a right. The futakuchi-onna's supernumerary mouth is often said to be unable to lie or sugarcoat opinions – to form the white lies that are part of many women's emotional toolboxes. The lips act as a verbalised id, stripped of super ego and ego, vocalising real thoughts, motivations and opinions.

So futakuchi-onna serve both as a cautionary tale for those who try to stop women from having a voice and inspirational figures for women yearning to express themselves – or eat in the way they need rather than what society or their families dictate. They're the yin to the body positive movement's yang; the stark warning that mournfully shadows singer–songwriter Megan Trainor's cheery 'All About the Bass' lyrics, proclaiming 'junk in all the right places'. In the last decade, women worldwide have started clapping back against the skinny girl hegemony: Lena Dunham and Beth Ditto are magazine cover girls, Rihanna's plus-size lingerie line is booming and Misty Copeland is a ballerina with booty – and they're not being quiet about it. They're marching into combat against the ghostly oppression of the futakuchi-onna and what she represents. Perhaps they may even at some point vanquish the need for her entirely.

CHAPTER FOUR

ELEMENTAL SPIRITS

Lightning bolt-throwers,
commanders of fire and ice,
creators of the planet

TIAMAT

BABYLONIAN: GODDESS

Also known as
Thaláttē
Tam-Tum

Nicknamed 'Chaos Monster', Babylonian goddess Tiamat brings drama and intensity to the party. This ancient, sea serpent deity was the mother of dragons, storms and fantastical beasts – a character straight out of *Game of Thrones* – and, so ancient Babylonians believed, the woman whose body was torn apart and used to create our world.

According to the *Enuma Elish*, the Babylonian creation myth written in 1900–1600 BCE, Tiamat spawned the earth. This story gets a little confusing, so strap yourself in. Babylonians believed that before the world existed, the universe consisted of seas. These seas were half sentient primordial entity, half deity; the female saltwater Tiamat, and the male fresh Apsu. When their waters mingled, they started to spawn gods, who went on to have more children – resulting in four generations in total. Tiamat's offspring were fantastical, among them the serpents Lahmu and Lahamu who parented Anshar and Kishar, heaven and earth. Anshar and Kishar gave birth to Anu – the sky and supreme god, Enki, the mischievous god of water and Enlil, the elemental god of storms, earth and wind. The younger kids were a pain; they played and argued, disturbing Apsu's sleep. So Apsu sought a solution from his adviser, Mummu. The plan they came up with was drastic; to kill these sons, daughters and grandchildren. On hearing of Apsu's plan, Tiamat was, rightfully, furious and warned great-grandchild Enki about the danger he was in. Enki captured Apsu, put him to sleep and, in a drastic move, killed him and stole his halo.

Although she had been cross about her consort Apsu's original plan, Tiamat was devastated by his death and declared war on her great-grandson Enki, as well as the rest of her children. She raised an army singlehandedly by spawning chimera, huge vipers, serpents 'merciless of fang', hurricanes, raging hounds, scorpion men, over-sized lions, mermen, bull-men and tempests. She married one of her deadly offspring, Kingu and installed him at the head of her beastly battalion.

However, Enki's son, Marduk, defied her. He volunteered to fight his great-grandmother on one condition – that on his victory, he was made king of the gods. He prepared by summoning huge, arrow-like winds to protect him.

He met his forebear on the battlefield. It was a scene soaked in high drama. The two walked warily towards each other, knowing this showdown had huge implications not just for their family, but on a worldwide scale. They started to fight. Marduk spread out his net, pinning the serpent goddess to the ground, as she helplessly flailed about. The winds that trailed furiously from his hands whined and twined around the pair, ear-splittingly loud. As his great-grandmother's mouth opened wide in a scream. Marduk directed his hurricanes between her lips – a none-too-subtle allegory for oral rape. In a grotesque echo of her pregnancies, the blast filled her belly, distending it.

Marduk took a spear and sliced her stomach open, ripping into her guts and organs, piercing her heart. He stood, victorious on her corpse, then smashed her skull and bled her dry. He then cleaved her body into two halves and, from them, fashioned the world, the stars, the moon. The story unfolded in gory, David Cronenberg-'body horror' style; her ribs used to make the vault of heaven and earth, her weeping eyes formed the huge Tigris and Euphrates rivers, her tail trailing off to become the Milky Way.

EVERYONE HAS A DYSFUNCTIONAL FAMILY

Tiamat's complex relationship with her children is fascinating to unpick. She's forced to take sides in a dysfunctional family, first confronting her husband's attitudes towards his rowdy offspring, but then later avenging him, even though this meant declaring war on her children. She's neither an out-and-out monster nor a bounteous earth mother, but somewhere between the two. Tied in a moral Gordian knot, she is forced to choose to show respect for her husband or protect her children. And that's a choice that results in her grisly death at the hands of her family. However, even as she is slaughtered, she brings the genesis of human existence, although in a very different manner to her initial creative procreation. She fashions the universe through birth, positivity and sacred love, but the human realm is built using her chaotic, hate-filled death, her rape, her body, her innards. It's almost a reversal of the birthing process; the mother's shell turned inside out, becoming shelter, sky, earth.

Tiamat's story has fascinated historians – author Robert Graves believed that the myth (like many similar god-vanquishes-goddess stories) represented the transition between a matriarchal and patriarchal society, that she embodied a long-forgotten female-dominated religion, her defeat and monstering a representation by the male successors of the quashing of this women-centric society and determination to demonise its leading lights. However, more recent historians, such as Lotte Motz in her *Faces of the Goddess* (1997) and Cynthia Eller in *The Myth of Matriarchal Prehistory* (2000), reject a wider prehistoric matriarchy as an 'ennobling lie'.

Whether or not she is a cypher for a deeper history, Tiamat is still an incredibly powerful and real representation of women. She's a goddess who commands monsters, invents water and slots stars and moons neatly into place. Yet she still has very mortal concerns; her kids are noisy, her husband complains and whines, her sons reach the stage where they start to stand up to their father. She, like many women, makes compromises in order to try to do the 'right thing'. Ultimately, she gives up her most precious possessions – the relationship with her children and her life – and through these sacrifices, creates earth. Perhaps, in the end, the 'chaos monster' commits the ultimate selfless act.

MAMI WATA

AFRICA/THE AMERICAS:
GODDESS

Also known as
Mammy Water
Mamy-Wata
Mawu-Lisu
Yemanja
Mamadilo
Maame Water
Watramama
La Sirène
Maman de l'Eau
and many more

The ultimate selfie-queen, you might find Mami Wata perched on a rock on a picture-perfect beach, grooming herself, peering into a mirror, pretending to be unaware of potential suitors until they're ensnared. She is deeply aware of the power of her own attractiveness – and is usually described in terms of excess, possessing an 'inhuman beauty' and unnaturally long hair. She loves material things, gadgets and disposable culture. A goddess tailor-made for the lifestyle-and-selfie world of Instagram.

In fact, Mami Wata was not originally singular. She was 'they', a pantheon of watery deities found in West, central and southern Africa, as well as in the African diaspora in the Americas and Caribbean. Mami Wata were overwhelmingly female, usually portrayed as half-human, half-fish creatures with thick hair. A complex blend of myth from across the continent, some believe they have their origins in ancient Egypt or Ethiopia; in Egypt *ma* or *mama* means 'truth and wisdom', while *wata* comes from *uati*, meaning

'ocean water' – some say Isis was originally worshipped under this name. Others maintain that the name was pidgin English for 'Mother Water'. In common with many mermaid myths, Mami may have had her origins in sailors' descriptions of incredible sea creatures, in this case, their tales of the elephantine manatee.

ALL ABOUT THE MONEY

From the fifteenth century onwards, the influence of European traders came to bear on the legend, codifying Mami's appearance and building her reputation. The traders brought gold, ships with figureheads depicting mermaids and told stories of mer-people and sirens, subtly altering the Mami Wata tale. In turn, they took her story with them as they travelled around the continent, spreading it to the corners of Africa. Perhaps because of the link between the traders and money, Mami Wata became associated with wealth.

Tales of her money-oriented deeds were innumerable. She snatched unwary swimmers, dragging them to her underwater kingdom, but when released, they were more attractive and had more cash. At other times, she was caught unawares on a riverbank, brushing her hair, and fled, dropping her mirror or comb. If a man took the item, he was haunted by Mami Wata in his dreams as she wheedled and demanded the return of her possessions. If he swore to be her faithful lover, she rewarded him with material goods, if not, she would curse him.

In other stories, she wandered market places, disguised as a beautiful woman, bedecked in jewellery. The traders' influence helped conjure Mami Wata into firm, singular existence. She had her own, distinctive form of worship; her followers created altars groaning with European goods and revelled in dances that led to a trance-like state. In Nigeria, her followers wore red to symbolise death, maleness and power, and white to represent wealth, beauty and femininity. Those same traders started to deal in humans. As thousands of enslaved Africans torn from different regions and tribes came together to work on slave plantations across the Atlantic Ocean, they mixed their various beliefs with Christianity and their traditional gods and goddesses began to absorb elements from other deities. People working unpaid in brutal conditions would perform the trance dance associated with the goddess in order to get them through the harsh ordeal of their lives and also as a healing ritual. By the seventeenth century, Mami Wata is thought to have mutated into Watra Mama found in Suriname's Winti religion, La Sirène in Haiti's Vodou and Yemanja in Brazil. She is also closely associated with Yemoja, another water spirit worshipped by the West African Yoruba people.

Back in Africa, the cult of Mami Wata continued to grow and change in different ways. In the 1880s, thousands of copies of a poster advertising a European freak show were printed and plastered on walls across West Africa. They showed an image of a snake charmer, thought to be Nala Damajanti, who gained fame touring with PT Barnum's circus. The poster caught the imagination of the population – immediately the image was absorbed into the collective consciousness and became entwined with the Mami Wata story. Her appearance was now set in stone. Henceforth, Mami Wata was depicted in Nala's image.

Mami Wata has remained a popular and commercial icon; she has been 'creolised' – blended with modern culture. The intriguing juxtaposition of this ancient, culturally and politically resonant goddess with her altars laden with objects more associated with Western capitalist society – designer sunglasses, cans of Coca-Cola, handbags and expensive make-up – makes for powerful imagery, imagery that has been seized by stylists, pop stars and artists. Female black singers have relished her luscious, watery look – space disco goddesses Labelle sang 'Lady Marmalade', dripping in wave-like feathers, Beyoncé alluded to her in her 'Lemonade' video and mermaid-obsessed Azealia Banks has pulled on a seashell G-string and let her hair cascade down her back as she dressed Mami-style, while hashtagging #mamiwata on Instagram. The goddess has also been the focus of major American art exhibitions, both experimental and traditional.

However, Mami Wata's popularity comes at a cost – African evangelical Christians and fundamentalist Muslims see her as a symbol of all that is wrong with modern life. They believe she uses her beauty cynically, she leads the vulnerable astray and she's materially focused. In addition, some see her as the ultimate post-capitalist goddess – as money and image obsessed as the most decadent hip-hop artist. Yet her confidence and kindness and connection to Mother Africa give her extra dimension for her newer fans. In short, she represents all that the older generation despise in the young, but frankly, the young don't care.

PELE

Even today, many native Hawaiians believe that Pele, the feared and revered deity of lava and volcanos, lives in the Halema'uma'u crater of the Kilauea peak on The Big Island. Each eruption on the island signifies Pele crying out for her true love. This strong, yet emotionally vulnerable goddess reserves particular ire for those who take pieces of lava from her precious volcanos, casting bad luck on the rock thieves. She is passionate about preserving her country.

Native Hawaiians believe in thousands of spirits, from gods that represent fertility, creation and war, to smaller deities that represented tides, flowers and even professions – it's thought that these beliefs are thousands of years old, although they were reinforced and codified by a wave of migrations from the Society Islands, c. 1000–1300 CE. Powerful Pele was the goddess of fire, lightning, violence and volcanos, one of six daughters and seven sons born to Haumea (the goddess of fertility and childbirth) and Kane Milohai (the creator of the sky and heavens). The family lived

in Kuaihelani, a mystical floating island, part of modern-day Tahiti. As a child, Pele's emotions always bubbled near the surface; she was passionate, jealous and capricious. One story telling how Pele ended up in Hawaii describes how she argued with her older sister, the sea goddess Nā-maka-o-Kahaʻi; they were like lava and water, hot and cold, steam spitting off hot rocks. The final straw came when Pele seduced her aquatic sister's husband. In fury, Kane Milohai banished his fiery goddess daughter from the island.

Luckily, Kamohoalii, Pele's shark god brother, was on hand to give her a ride in his canoe. They took some of their siblings with them, including an egg containing Pele's baby sister Hi'iaka, which she tucked safely under her armpit. The family headed south, but their journey was ardous as they had to face the wrath of Nā-maka-o-Kahaʻi, their trip becoming a battle against their ocean-controlling sister. Every time they tried to land and dig a pit for their home, Nā-maka-o-Kahaʻi angrily flooded it.

Eventually, the group made it to Hawaii, where Pele used her divining stick to help find a good place to live – she first tried Kauai, but was attacked by her ocean-dwelling sister. Pele recovered and limped to Oahu, where she dug craters in Honolulu, then Molkai and Maui, where she raised the Haleakala volcano. Pele was a hard worker, hewing natural features into her native landscape. It was in Maui that the sisters met again, battling for the final time. Nā-maka-o-Kahaʻi tore her sister limb from limb, her bones forming the hill of Ka-iwi-o-Pele. Her spirit flew on, however, and created a home in the Halema'uma'u crater at the top of the Kilauea volcano, where you'll still find her today.

Other stories tell how she had a short, tempestuous relationship with Kamapuaa, the pig-man god of water – their violent battles symbolised the destructive capabilities of a hydrovolcanic eruption. Pele was brokenhearted when he jumped into the ocean and left her, believing her dead. Further tales have the hot-tempered goddess throwing molten lava at rivals and lovers, transforming them into pillars of rock. These stories were documented in writing, most notably in the nineteenth century, but were almost lost when America outlawed the teaching of the Hawaiian language in 1896.

PELE'S INFLUENCE TODAY

Pele is still present in every corner of Hawaii, however – paintings of her dressed in trademark red hang on shop walls, and you can buy volcano goddess snowstorms in tourist shops. When the mountain starts to rumble – it's one of the most active in the world – you'll find offerings to the goddess, flowers, money, incense or palm lily leaves, stuffed in the cracks near the summit of the volcano. When it erupts, gifts left to appease the goddess stand forlornly on the front steps of abandoned houses in the path of the lava, while the strands of volcanic glass that drift from the fissure are named 'Pele's hair'. Every eruption throws up new YouTube videos that claim to show the goddess' face in the lava flow. Pele is said to shape shift, to appear as a beautiful young maid or elderly woman to reward those who are generous and punish those who are greedy.

Her flames flicker more widely too; Tori Amos' 1996 album *Boys for Pele* is named after her and contains numerous references to the patriarchal nature of religion and the heat of female power, while characters based on her appear in programmes as diverse as *Sabrina the Teenage Witch* and, inevitably, *Hawaii 5-0*.

Pele is an inspirational figure; passionate, incredibly strong, a goddess who literally formed her own country, her life events sculpting and forming the islands. She has her human side – serious daddy issues, a raging temper, a complicated love life. You might imagine her today hogging the headlines, her relationships messy and very, very public, soul-baring travelogue posts spilling out across social media. Perhaps it's this barely contained emotion that ensures she's still worshipped as a strong, vital goddess, still as venerated today as she was thousands of years ago – just like a volcano, she is unconquerable.

SELKIES

SCOTTISH: CREATURES

Also known as
Silkies
Sylkies
Selchies
Selkie folk
Maighdeann-mhara
Marmennlar
Finns

Torn from their underwater life, these northern Scottish-linked half-seal creatures have families and responsibilities on land, yet remain yoked to the sea. Ultimately, no human can tame selkies, so their return to the depths is inexorable; they crave an elemental and wild life.

Although there are male selkies, it is the females who are at the centre of the most compelling tales that swirl about the islands of Shetland and Orkney. The large grey seals found basking lazily on rocks and bobbing like tapioca pearls in the grey waves were thought to cast off their heavy fur skins every Midsummer Eve to dance, carefree on the shore. The creatures' expressive, mournful eyes and baby-like cries would only have reinforced the idea that they were almost human.

According to tales told around fireplaces in winter, if a man steals the skin of a selkie, she is compelled to become his wife, and as long as the skin remains hidden from her, she is bound to her husband. There are myriad stories of selkie women who have a life on shore, married with children, but remain compelled by the sea, spending hours and days on blustery cliffs, staring hungrily at the waves. However strong the bond is with their new family, the compulsion to return to the depths is more powerful – they commonly only survive seven years on land, where a selkie may grow thin and weak and start to dry out. If a selkie woman can find her skin, she is allowed to return to her seabed home, abandoning her land-bound life. Often a child may innocently lead her to her coat, threadbare, hidden in the eaves of the roof or in a locked sea chest. Or a seal-woman's aquatic sisters might emerge from the waves, bringing with them a new skin. Some selkies are said to return to visit their family subsequently, and others appear to their children as mournful seals, but most simply disappear back under the waves, their fate unknown.

A CAUTIONARY TALE

The tragic-romantic nature of the selkie tale lends itself to storytelling, song and film and has been reworked in popular culture, including, memorably, by Joan Baez in her cover of the traditional folk song 'Silkie', in the Irish animation Song of the Sea and in Joanna Newsom's song 'Colleen', in which an ex-selkie, unable to remember her life before the island, assumes she was a criminal, but is reminded of her old life by a sailor and dives back into the depths of the sea.

The themes of these stories perhaps resonate most deeply with women. The ensnaring of the seal-women as wives emerged in a sparsely populated area at a time of patriarchal structure, which meant women had less choice about who they married. Selkies serve as cautionary tales for both men and women: you may thrust domesticity, a family, and other responsibilities on a woman who wants a more carefree life or who has been torn from her childhood home, but beware, as she may be restless for her previous existence and leave.

The symbolism of the sea is important. Temperamental waters can shift from dark fury to sparkling calm in minutes. Compared to the solid shore, the ocean is elemental, a place to truly be free, to float, to lose oneself, to find your soul and centre. No wonder these women, with their domestic and emotional responsibilities, have always pined for the waves, find them calling on a deep level. Everyone needs time out to recharge, but if a woman is denied this (or denies it herself), then eventually something will snap. Perhaps selkies were early symbols of the virtues of self-care and mindfulness, a reminder to husbands to 'let' their women run free a little.

The stories also make incarnate a deeper longing. The stealing of the skin could be seen to represent a woman losing a vital part of herself when she enters a union and starts a family. That taking on the day-to-day needs of a household or husband could mean she must give up going out, cast off her old friends, and relinquish her own interests as she pulls on a new mantle of caring for a home and children. But folded in the attic lies the skin, the embodiment of her old life, charged with potential.

As she gets older, that skin's youthful appeal and possibilities starts to exert a powerful attraction. And the woman, with maturity, becomes more confident, and her children rely on her less and less. Should she pull on her old coat and vanish back into the freedom of the waves, the freedom of her past life? Can a husband ever 'tame' a truly vibrant, elemental woman? Or will she always find her old sealskin, shake off her responsibilities and dive back into glorious wildness?

MARI

Also known as
Mari Urraca
Anbotoko Mari
Murumendiko Dama

Elemental, bounteous and supportive, Mari is the mother goddess of the Basque region that straddles areas of south-west France and north-central Spain. But is she also the wrinkled, last-standing reminder of a long-lost, pan-European goddess-worshipping religion?

Worshipped in pre–Christian times but still acknowledged today, Mari is the goddess of the elements – hail, rain, storms and droughts. She also personified the earth, making her home in the network of caves that honeycombed both beneath the Basque country and through mountains, many of them opulently decorated in gold. She was married to the Sugaar, a serpent-type god who also lived underground. The two met every Friday afternoon when Sugaar would brush Mari's hair amid hail and rain storms.

Even today, Mari's activities correspond with the elements. Every town's Mari has slightly different characteristics. For example, in the towns of Oñati and Aretxabaleta, in the Basque region of northern Spain, they claim that when Mari is on Mount Anboto, it rains, but when she is on the nearby Aloña limestone formation, it is dry. Her descriptions also vary from town to town. She is known to pull clouds out of a cave and create storms, to suck winds from wells and throw them across valleys. If she bakes bread or does her laundry, a cloud of smoke might emerge from her cave. In common with many other European goddesses, she's also associated with spinning, using gold yarn or winding her thread around a ram's horns.

Mari's servants are lamiñak – duck-footed humanoid creatures – and sorguiñ – nocturnal witches who collect tithes for their mistress. If you visit her, you are forbidden to sit down, have to address her with the familiar pronoun *tú* and are forbidden to turn your back on her. She is a strict goddess, condemning lying, greediness, lack of respect and theft, which she punishes through sending hailstorms, stealing property in return or merely inflicting a guilty conscience. However, Mari is also caring. Basques lost in the wilderness still know today to call her name three times. On the third shout, their goddess will perch on their head and show them the way back to civilisation.

THE CINDY SHERMAN OF GODDESSES

Most commonly depicted wearing a red dress, with a halo of stars or the moon, Mari takes many other forms – she's the Cindy Sherman of goddesses, famed for her use of make-up, props and prosthetics in the creation of multiple imagined characters. Mari will often have hooved feet. Sometimes she'll be driving a carriage drawn through the air by horses, riding a ram or shooting fire from her hands. In other regions, she manifests as animals, a vulture, a raven, a horse or a goat. She's also taken on more abstract appearances, a gust of wind, a white cloud or a rainbow.

However she looks, Mari isn't shy; there are thousands of tales of her appearances. One well-known story tells of a young orphan shepherdess who had lost one of her flock. Panicking, she went to find the missing sheep. Despite knowing how dangerous it was to approach Mari's cave, the girl strayed near, looking for her woolly charge. 'At the entrance of the cavern, she saw a beautiful woman she knew to be Mari. She asked the orphaned girl to come and live with her, saying that if she did, she would make her rich. After seven years of life with the goddess, learning about spinning, breadmaking, herbalism and the language of animals, the girl was let go, Mari giving her a huge lump of coal. Her protégée was a little disappointed, but hid her grumpiness well. As soon as she left the cave, however, the black rock turned into a shining nugget of gold, so big that it paid for a house and a flock of sheep and enabled the girl to live an independent, happy life. This heartwarming tale portrays Mari as a goddess who not only gave short-term help, but checked her privilege to elevate women who didn't come from a position of power to break the glass ceiling. She provided the girl with an education as well as the means to live independently of men – she had a new life, but also interests and skills outside of domestic duties with which to fill it.

When enforced mass conversions to Christianity took place in the Basque region in the tenth and eleventh centuries CE, Mari's status was downgraded, folded into the new religion. Some claim that elements of Mari were absorbed into Jesus' mother, Mary, in order to soften the move towards Christianity. However, even after the area was fully Christianised, priests said mass at the entrance of Mari's cave and offerings were made to ensure a bounteous harvest; still many people believe in her powers in parallel with their Christian worship. Some historians assert that although Christianity came to be the dominant religion, the geographical and social isolation of the Basque region meant that it acted as an airlock for Mari, representing the last vestiges of the Neolithic, pan-European goddess cult – a religion based around megalithic structures, the spinning of fate and the cycles of birth–life–death, maiden–mother–crone, spring–harvest–winter. The idea of Mari sitting, staring through rheumy eyes out of her cave, a millennia-upon-millennia-old goddess in her twilight years, weaving the fate of her people with crinkled fingers, but still kept alive through veneration and dwindling sacrifices is a little tragic, yet deeply romantic.

THE LADY OF LLYN Y FAN FACH

WELSH: FAIRY

A far cry from any Disney fairy, the straight-talking Nelferch, better known as The Lady of Llyn y Fan Fach, gives us a schooling in ultimatums, boundaries and consequences.

This Celtic lady takes her name from a real place, Llyn y Fan Fach, a mirror-like, 25-acre lake on the edge of the Welsh Black Mountains in the Brecon Beacons National Park. There are countless stories of fairies and water in Celtic culture – the border between fairyland and our realm is said to be at its thinnest around water. Water worship was part of druidism; wells, springs and streams could all be holy, places of healing – kings were even required to swear in their posts near a body of water. Nelferch was one of the Gwragedd Annwn – Welsh water fairies who lived in submerged palaces. And there are echoes of Nelferch's story in the Arthurian Lady-in-the-Lake story.

Ancient fairies were a far cry from the plastic doll-like figures we often think of today. They were other-worldly, of course, but with a rich, intricate society of their own. Across Celtic cultures and beyond, the term 'fairies' was often used in place of 'gods' and 'goddesses' by religious writers who anthologised earlier polytheistic tales to soften the deities. Across Ireland, Scotland and Wales, the 'fairies' were the last vestiges of pre-Christian gods and goddesses. In Celtic lore, humans were free to enter fairyland, but often found its rules confusing.

'Wild women aren't to be tamed, their relationship boundaries are to be respected, lest they disappear back into the water.'

Many earthly families claimed to be of fairy descent – a claim that acted to legitimise and empower clans. Other-worldly ancestry was also part of many other cultures – the Egyptian pharaohs, the Norse and Irish kings all claimed lineage to gods.

THE YOUNG MAN OF MYDDFAI

Nelferch's story, told in many variations from the tenth to the twenty-first century, begins with Gwyn, a young farm boy who lived with his mother in Myddfai and liked to take his cattle to graze near the lake, which lay a couple of hours walk from his home. One morning, he caught sight of a beautiful woman, sitting on a rock, brushing her hair with a golden comb. He offered her some home-baked, slightly hard bread, but she laughed at him and jumped into the water, disappearing beneath the surface. The next day, he took softer bread with him. Again, the ethereally lovely woman was at the lakeside and, although she smiled encouragingly, she once again dived away.

The bread Gwyn baked that night was perfect. This time Nelferch took it, smiling, and stepped ashore. 'I will wed you,' she said, 'and I will live with you until I receive from you *tri ergyd diachos* – three blows without a cause.' She told him that when he struck the third blow, she would leave him forever. Gwyn agreed to her terms and the girl dived into the lake one last time. Rather disconsolate, Gwyn was shocked when he turned away from the water to see three figures standing before him – a regal-looking old man and two identical-looking women, one with whom he'd fallen in love. The man told Gwyn to pick out Nelferch. Gwen's heart leaped as he recognised a flaw in her sandal and picked her out. The man promised to give the pair as many animals as his daughter could ask for without pausing for breath. Nelferch's hours spent diving underwater paid off – and she named enough livestock to fill a farm. The couple married and went on to have three sons. One day, the couple were walking to a wedding at the church in Myddfai. Nelferch was dawdling so Gwyn flicked her playfully with his gloves. Nelferch turned to him and in an emotionless tone said, 'That was your first blow.' Distraught, Gwyn vowed never to touch his wife unexpectedly again.

Years later, while at a christening, Nelferch burst uncontrollably into tears and Gwyn put his hand on her shoulder to comfort her. She whispered, 'I was crying because I could see into the child's future – he's not long for this world, and his short life will be painful. Oh, and another thing, that was your second blow.' The child subsequently died and Nelferch and Gwyn attended his funeral. Halfway through the ceremony, Nelferch let out a peal of happy laughter. Gwyn was horrified, and tapped her on the back. 'I was laughing because I can see the child, whole again, healthy, and living in a better place,' explained Nelferch, 'And that, husband, was your third.' She stood up abruptly and walked out of the church. Gwyn followed, watching helplessly as she strode through their farm, calling the animals to her, each following her down to the lake. There she and the livestock walked into the water and disappeared beneath the surface without a backward glance.

Gwyn and their sons were distraught; the boys went to the lake every day to weep for their lost mother, until one morning, miraculously, she came striding from the water. She had purpose, to teach her children the intricacies of herbalism and healing. Thanks to her magical knowledge, the boys went on to become famous doctors: The Physicians of Myddfai, who cured lords and became rich landowners themselves. Their remedies are included in the fourteenth-century collection of Welsh tales, *Red Book of Hergest* – also the source for the *Mabinogion* story cycle (see Rhiannon, pages 42–45) held today at Jesus College, Oxford.

Nelferch has agency, choosing when she will agree to the marriage and setting, very clearly, the terms for it. She will not stand for abuse of any kind, intended or otherwise and sticks rigidly to those terms. She earns her own dowry and regards the animals as her property, taking them with her when she returns to the lake. She chooses when to return to earth and is focused on imparting knowledge to her sons, teaching them in order to help society and provide them with a living. Her story echoes the lesson the selkies (see pages 148–51) taught: that wild women aren't to be tamed, that their relationship boundaries are to be respected, lest they disappear back into the water. In addition, Nelferch's uncompromising approach is a lesson in communication, in being straightforward about your needs.

THE RAINBOW SERPENT

ABORIGINAL AND TORRES STRAIT ISLANDERS, AUSTRALIA: GENDER-FLUID GODDESS/GOD

Also known as
Ungud
Wagyl
Wonambi
Yulunggal

A gender-fluid god-figure, the Rainbow Serpent acts on a huge scale. According to one of the oldest surviving civilizations on earth, she created the landscape, but also represents something more human, the tricky transition from child to adult.

In a country as parched as Australia, a rainbow, signifying rainfall, is one of the most welcome sights. Many tribes believe that the coloured arch is a representation of the deity snaking across the sky from one waterhole to another. So this god-figure represents both life and death. She brings fertility, crops and sustenance, but, if she's angry and withholds the supply, famine and destruction stalk the red earth.

There are believed to be many separate rainbow serpents found in the stories of the Aboriginal and Torres Strait Islanders of mainland Australia.

Sometimes female, sometimes male, often ambiguously gendered (a man with breasts), the rainbow serpent is known by myriad names: Ungud, Wagyl, Wonambi, Yulunggal. Yet they share similar characteristics in many of the stories. Her stories have been told for at least 6,000 years and are set in the 'everywhen', a concept of past, present and future difficult to convey in Western language.

The Rainbow Serpent is a vital part of the Aboriginal creation myth, the 'Dreamtime'. She created the landscape of the country. It's said that she coursed through the earth, travelling between sources of water, throwing up mountains and gorges in her wake. Her slithering created valleys and hills, lakes and bays formed where she rested. She fashioned the waterways, the geological features that held the most vital natural resource; without her, there would be only flat desert. Aboriginal and Torres Strait Islanders believe that the serpent still lives in water: oceans, waterfalls, salt and fresh.

SLITHER AND SWALLOW

The Rainbow Serpent plays an important role in the Aboriginal myth of the Wawalag sisters – Waimariwi and Boaliri. They are descendents of the Djanggawul – a trio of creation deities. There are many variations on the tale, but key points are shared. The two siblings are journeying from their home near the Roper River to the northern coast. The older sister – Waimariwi – is heavily pregnant, so progress is slow. One evening, the pair stop to rest, and the elder sister's waters break – the birth has begun. Calmly, Boaliri builds her a hut in which to have her baby, and the pair begin the birthing ritual, singing songs and dancing. Some of Waimariwi's blood flows from the hut, trickling towards a nearby waterhole. A waterhole in which, unbeknown to the pair, the Rainbow Serpent is lurking. As the blood reaches the water, the Rainbow Serpent awakens, angry that her home has been defiled.

She sends a great storm. Lightning flashes around the hut and thunder roars, and the sisters raise their voices and chant louder to match the noise. The Rainbow Serpent rouses herself from her watering hole and enters the hut, swallowing the girls and their baby. However, as well as the sisters, the serpent has also eaten a little ant, who twitches and irritates the snake's stomach until she vomits up the family. But this salvation is short-lived. The snake eats the girls again, then raises herself to her full height and begins a conversation with the other great snakes of the country. She tells them of all the things she has consumed, and finally admits to eating the sisters. Finally, she lowers herself back into the hole, the sisters still lodged inside.

This intensely Freudian tale forms the basis of rituals for Aboriginal people. For them, the Wawalag sisters' story concerns bleeding and female menstruation, particularly the ability of women to synchronise their periods. Starting to menstruate is a sign that you're becoming ready to have children, an important event that is marked by the Aboriginal people with the Kunapipi blood ritual. While Western cultures are just catching on to the concept of 'Red Tent' parties and celebrations to mark a girl's first period, ancient civilisations have been practising their own versions for millennia. This important time puts aboriginal women on the same footing as the serpent – they are now creators, they can bring life, and that's a cause for celebration.

The tale also forms the basis of a coming-of-age ritual for boys, which involves dancing, the playing of the didgeridoo, and sacred blood-letting and use of menstrual blood. The men symbolically 'menstruate' and 'give birth', while participants are painted with red ochre designs that represent the serpent. The Rainbow Serpent is placed in charge of one of the most crucial stages in a man's life; the transition from boy to man. This responsibility is huge; raising children to be respectful and teaching that they don't need to conform to gender norms and that they should be kind is vital to the future of society. But luckily, the Aboriginal and Torres Strait Islanders have a rainbow-coloured, gender-fluid snake on hand to help.

This multi-coloured creature is an iconic part of modern Australian culture too. Dick Roughsey's book, *The Rainbow Serpent*, is a childhood staple, while the annual Rainbow Serpent electronic music festival has brought her tale to ravers in Melbourne. The combination of ancient myth and contemporary issues that the snake represents is potent; she's become a symbol for ecological groups in Australia and across the world, and LGBT+ Australians, particularly those of Aboriginal and Torres Strait Islander origins. And so this 6,000-year-old gender-fluid goddess slithers comfortably between old worlds and new, finding her place in every generation.

MAZU

**MAZUISM/BUDDHISM/
TAOISM/CONFUCIANISM:
GODDESS**

Also known as
Mat-su, Mazupo, A-ma
Linghui Furen
Linghui Fei
Tianfei
Huguo Bimin Miaoling Zhaoying
   Hongren Puji Tianfei
Tianhou
Tianshang Shengmu
Tongxian Lingnu
Shennu
Zhaoxiao Chunzheng Fuji
   Ganying Shengfei

One of the most worshipped goddesses in the world – over 200 million people are believed to follow her – Mazu has her roots in the extraordinary, real-life Lin Mo-Niang, who lived in the tenth century.

Born in 960 CE to a fishing family who lived on Meizhou Island in the straits of Taiwan, off the coast of south-eastern China, Lin Mo-Niang arrived to a room flooded with light and filled with the heady scent of fresh flower blossoms. Mo-Niang was an exceptional young girl; she was extremely clever and had a photographic memory.

At the age of four, she visited a temple and was tranfixed by a picture of Guanyin, a bodhisattva known for her compassion. Mo-Niang became a fervent Buddhist and was given the gift of being able to foresee the future. She devoured religious texts and studied with a priest, Xuantong, who taught her the art of translocation, which she sneakily used to visit private gardens near her house, wandering among the flowers. In her teens, she became a keen swimmer and developed a love of the ocean. She would help guide her fisher family home, wearing red so they could spot her through the thick mists that swirled around the island, and once even set her own house on fire in order to signal a boat into shore.

At this point, Mo-Niang's tale becomes more mystical. When she was fifteen, she and two friends used a pool as a mirror to admire their new dresses. Out of nowhere, a giant sea creature burst from the depths, brandishing a bronze medallion. While her terrified friends ran away, Mo-Niang accepted the disc, which granted her supernatural powers. Powers that were put to good use.

One dark and stormy afternoon, Mo-Niang's brothers and father were out fishing. Mo-Niang was at home, weaving a tapestry, when she fell into a trance. She had a vision of her family, their boat tossed on the gigantic waves and capsizing. She used her powers of teleportation to reach them, fighting to keep them all above the surface. She managed to support them all, gripping her father in her teeth. However, back at home, her mother noticed Mo-Niang's body slumped against her loom and, disastrously, woke her, leaving her father at the mercy of the ocean. When her brothers returned, they told her that her father had been lost. Distraught, Mo-Niang walked into the sea, where she took three days to find his body.

> 'I have no fear of depths and a great fear of shallow living.'
> –ANAÏS NIN, *THE FOUR-CHAMBERED HEART*

Mo-Niang refused to marry; when she received proposals from two generals she insisted they fight her for the privilege. The pair, highly skilled in martial arts, were defeated – some say they killed each other, others claim they were whipped by the girl herself – an expert in kung fu. Spoiler alert – they went on to become Mo-Niang's sidekick demons when she transformed into a goddess. Other stories tell how the generals were already in demonic form, and simply tamed by Mo-Niang, using a magical silk scarf.

Mo-Niang died relatively young, at twenty-eight. Accounts of her death vary, but the most romantic is that one day she simply said goodbye to her family and climbed to the top of a mountain near her home. There, at the foggy summit, she dived into the mists, arcing up towards heaven, flying on a rainbow to become a goddess. After her death, the people of the island built a temple to their friend and brand new goddess, renamed Mazu. She became the patron goddess of the sea, protecting sailors and her worship spread quickly. Temples sprung up across what is now China and Taiwan, decked with statues of Mazu in her trademark red robe. This compassionate goddess contrasted with the stern father figures of the day such as the Dragon Kings. Perhaps it was this empathy that made her so popular. She was promoted dozens times over the next thousand years, and absorbed other, smaller goddesses until she became 'Heavenly Empress'. Mazuism is a stand-alone religion, although there are also shrines to her at Buddhist and Tao temples.

FROM STRENGTH TO STRENGTH

Despite fewer people relying on dangerous fishing to earn a living, Mazuism continues to grow – there are almost twice as many Mazu temples in Taiwan now as in 1980, and many more worldwide, from Melbourne to San Francisco. A temporary bamboo Mazu temple, topped with a 40ft lotus, was even built at the US Burning Man festival in 2015.

It's said that people in trouble will call on Mazu before any other god – she doesn't have to pull on a fancy dress or look in a mirror before running to help. She's a domestic goddess, known informally as 'mother' or 'granny' among ordinary people. Families have Mazu shrines in their house and fishermen icons on their boats. Women who live on her island fashion their hair, Mazu-style, into sail shapes and wear half-red trousers in tribute to their heroine.

Once virulently anti-religion, China's Communist Party is now encouraging the staging of events such as the Mazu pilgrimage held in China's third lunar month, although they are careful to describe it as a celebration of cultural heritage rather than worship. Perhaps the democratic nature of Mazu's temples temper the religious aspect for the party – ordinary people tend them and anyone can declare themselves a believer – there are no initiation ceremonies or creeds to learn. The fact that the celebrations also bring tourists, Taiwanese trade and money to the country probably also helps.

So Mazu has made the journey from the simple daughter of a fishing family to international renown with temples worldwide. One can only wonder what a four-year-old Lin Mo-Niang would make of it all. Ironically, for a figure so rooted in a communist country, she could be seen to be completing the ultimate capitalist journey, the American Dream, as she makes her way from nothing to inspiring the world.

EGLĖ THE QUEEN OF SERPENTS

LITHUANIAN: WOMAN

The Romeo-and-Juliet-style story of Eglė and her serpent prince is romantic and tragic, but has a tree-transformation twist. Eglė might be the epitome of woman-as-chattel, but her speedy thinking, sisterly attitude and self-determination has inspired and comforted young Lithuanians for centuries.

Eglė's story is part of the canon of Lithuanian fairy tales. The country was one of the last European countries to convert to Christianity at the end of the fourteenth century, so their god and goddess myths sing brightly from their folk stories, barely concealed by the thin layer of fireside sugar coating.

Eglė was a farmer's daughter, the youngest of twelve. Dressing after a day of swimming with her sisters, she was shocked to find a grass snake trapped in her sleeve. The serpent protested in a man's voice, 'Eglė! Become my bride and I'll get out of here!' Eglė, in a panic, agreed, and the snake slithered off.

Three days later, the family's garden had become a sea of thousands of twisting, writhing snakes. They hissed, 'We want Eglė; she has promised.' Eglė's parents were adamant, no snakes were taking their daughter. Her father tried to fool the reptiles, by giving them, in turn, a goose, sheep and cow dressed in his daughter's clothes. But, each time, a cuckoo gave the snakes warning. Finally, the beasts threatened the farm with ruin and, sadly, the farmer gave in and handed his daughter over.

They slithered her back to the lake, where a handsome young man awaited. Her snake had transformed into a prince, Žilvinas. The pair fell madly in love, made a home under the sea and had four children. One day Eglė asked her husband permission to visit her childhood home. Žilvinas was reluctant to let her go, fearful she might never return, so set her three tasks in succession: to spin an infinite amount of silk, to wear a pair of iron shoes until they wore down, and to bake a cake – after he had hidden every kitchen utensil in the kingdom bar one. Seeking advice from an old woman, Eglė used cunning to complete every challenge so, reluctantly, the prince let her leave. He told her to utter a special charm when she wanted to come home: 'Žilvinas! If you are alive, send waves of milk, if not, send waves of blood.'

Eglė returned to the farm with her children. She told her family about her blissful new life, but her brothers wanted her to stay and plotted to take her back by force. They intimidated Eglė's children, trying to learn the secret chant that would bring Žilvinas to the surface and finally, the youngest, Drubele, cracked and whispered the words. The men went to the lake, and shouted the enchanted words. The serpent prince came to the surface and the brothers brutally hacked him to death with their scythes. The next morning, Eglė went to the lake and called for her beloved, but was greeted by a bloody foam. The voice of her husband whispered in her ear, telling her who had killed him and who had betrayed her – her own daughter. Waves of grief and fury engulfed her and she gathered her weeping, terrified children and, using magic, one-by-one, she turned them into trees. Her three sons became an oak, an ash and a birch and her daughter a shivering aspen. Finally, with tears streaming down her face, she turned herself into a spruce – the evergreen, resilient tree that blankets the mountains of Lithuania and still bears the name Eglė.

Her tragic story can be seen, on one level, as a simple creation myth, explaining how trees were formed and named. It's also significant that grass snakes play such an important role in the tale; they were symbols of fertility and wealth and kept as pets in Lithuanian households.

A GLOBAL PHENOMENON

The saga is thought to have travelled from India via Kazakhstan and Ukraine to Lithuania, where it was first documented in 1837, and went on to inspire artworks, plays, exhibitions. In 1940, it formed the basis of a hugely popular poem by Lithuanian poet Salomėja Nėris, a work whose themes of betrayal and migration foreshadowed the Second World War. Is it any wonder though that, even in its infancy, this tale journeyed so far and resonated with so many women from so many cultures?

At its root, the story is about attitudes towards women. It was shared domestically at a time when women were seen as property to be bartered for power or financial gain. Terrified at the thought of losing their home, Eglė's family traded their daughter for their own future security. Then, after she fell in love with the creature they sent her to, she was punished again; her husband slaughtered by her own brothers. This has echoes of modern-day 'honour killings' in which women are killed for being rape victims or for refusing arranged marriages.

On another level, the story is about the threat of marriage which, in the past – and in some places, the present – hung quivering above the heads of young girls. The fear that they could be married off to an older, intimidating suitor at a young age, that they would be uprooted from their familial home and thrust into a strange place where they would be expected to keep a house and sleep with someone they barely knew – those slithering snakes couldn't be more Freudian.

> 'When a woman teams up with a snake a moral storm threatens somewhere.'
> – STACY SCHIFF,
> *CLEOPATRA, A LIFE*

However, Eglė would have given these terrified girls some hope. She was, of course, lucky that her husband turned out to be handsome and kind. She also displayed a growing resilience as she matured. She becomes the director of her own story, gaining agency and even her final, tragic act was on her terms.

In *From The Beast to The Blonde* (1994), feminist Marina Warner asserts: 'Fairy tales exchange knowledge between an older voice of experience and a younger audience, they present pictures of perils and possibilities that lie ahead... They stand up to adversity with dreams of vengeance, power and vindication.' Eglė's tale has 'perils and possibilities' in spades. However she rolls up her sleeves and attempts to find practical solutions to her problems, even if some of those solutions are shocking.

CHAPTER FIVE

MUNIFICENT SPIRITS

Bountiful deities, generous
spirits, domestic goddesses

TĀRĀ

Also known as
Ārya Tārā
Jetsun Dölma
Tara Bosatsu
Duōluó Púsà
Wisdom Moon

Goddess Tārā's refusal to transform into male form in order to achieve enlightenment is a masterclass in self belief. Recognised across Hinduism and absorbed into many strands of Buddhism as goddess, bodhisattva and Buddha, Tārā remains immensely popular in Tibet and Mongolia. A little confusingly, she has several derivation tales. She may have had her roots in Shaktism – a precursor to Hinduism – where she was seen as a mother goddess.

Tārā was first referred to by name in the *Mañjuśrī-mūla-kalpa*, written around the fifth century CE. But perhaps her most inspiring origin story was written in India around 700–80 CE. This was a time of major changes in Buddhism, as different strands of the religion were forming what eventually became Vajrayana – a form of the belief that encourages its followers to relive the experiences of the founder of Buddhism. The contribution from and importance of women to religion was becoming more acknowledged, as they emerged as both teachers and Buddhas.

WISDOM MOON

According to the Origin of Tara Tantra, Tārā was first known as Wisdom Moon, a devout princess. The bright, sparky royal studied hard, made dutiful offerings and was close to reaching enlightenment (achieving the higher knowledge of a Buddha). At last, she came before the Buddha and took her bodhisattva vow – a promise of her intent to remain on the path to Buddhahood and to elevate the needs of others above her own. It immediately became apparent to the monks present that Wisdom Moon was something special, a high achiever. They congratulated her, then explained that if she prayed to be reborn, reincarnated as a man, then she might attain enlightenment. Tārā smiled, jutted out her chin and retorted: 'Here there is no man; there is no woman, no self, no person, and no consciousness. Labelling 'male' or 'female' is hollow. Oh, how worldly fools delude themselves'. She went on to make a defiant vow: 'Those who wish to attain supreme enlightenment in a man's body are many, but those who wish to serve the aims of beings in a woman's body are few indeed; therefore may I, until this world is emptied out, work for the benefit of all humans in a woman's body.' And that she did. She was reborn in female form, going on to meditate for 10,100,000 years, and consequently to release the same number of beings from the bondage of their worldly minds. Through this toil she became a goddess – Tārā.

In another Tibetan Buddhism tale, Tārā sprang from a lotus that grew in the tears of Avalokitesvara (also known as Chenrezig), the compassionate Buddha. He was crying because he recognised that all of humankind was suffering, yet there was little he could do to help. Full of energy, Tārā offered to help him ease the pain of the world. But Tārā has become more than a sidekick to a male Buddha or another interchangeable goddess. A master of travel and navigation, she has helped people navigate choppy waters, both physical and spiritual and is also known as a forest deity. Most important is her capacity for instant, compassionate, unconditional action – she's often represented with one leg drawn inward, as if in meditation, but the other outstretched, literally ready to strike out. She dives straight in to help, no questions asked, with no discrimination, caring for all humankind fiercely, as if each were her child. Today you could imagine her at the front of a climate change demonstration, a fierce green mother earth warrior, placard in hand, urging people on, but, at the same time being watchful that everyone else is safe.

A GODDESS OF MANY GUISES

Tārā takes many forms. In some strands of Buddhism, she has twenty-one guises, each associated with a different colour and with different characteristics: Green Tārā, the saviour and most prominent of the group; White Tārā, the healer who represents long life; Red Tārā, who uses her powers of attraction to find people to help; the wealth form of Yellow Tārā; Blue Tārā, the wrathful warrior and Black Tārā, full of power and who manifests via a secret mantra. This rainbow of Tārās brings subtlety and shades of meaning to her character – those who have complex requirements can draw on exactly the right combination of Tārās they need. This multiplicity is one of Tārā's most endearing attributes; she can be contrary and embodies the complexities of many women's lives, balancing home and work, being assertive or caring, rent maker, homebody, fighter, protector.

Tārā's tale has inspired women across thousands of years of Buddhism. She has served to encourage Buddhists to not just sit and meditate, but to get up and do, to be immediately present and full of action. Buddhist communities worldwide name temples after the goddess and include Tārā rituals or practices as part of their devotions. Ultimately, there's something very earthly and real about this goddess who not only insisted on staying in her female form, but serves to embody the complexities and can-do spirit of women everywhere.

MADDERAKKA

Also known as
Madder-Akka
Mattarakka
Maadteraahka

Childbirth can be an intimidating prospect –
even more so in a pre-anaesthetic or antibiotic
age. Luckily, for the Sámi – who live in Sápmi,
a region that encompasses parts of Norway,
Sweden, Finland and Russia – Madderakka and
her three daughters Sarakka, Juksakka and
Uksakka are there to guide women through
the turmoil.

In the Sámi language, 'Akka' means great grandmother,
and there is a pantheon of 'akka' spirits associated
with birth and death. Madderakka, the mother
goddess, is responsible for the safe delivery of babies.
She lives under the floor of the Sámi huts, in the earth.
In one birth myth, her companion, Madderatcha, the
god of humanity, creates souls, then passes these on
to Madderakka who cloaks them each in a body. In
another story, the supreme god, Radien, creates a
soul and gives it to Madderatcha who carries it in his
belly, making a trip around the sun before giving it to
Madderakka. She then gives the baby to Sarakka, if
it is a girl, and to Juksakka, if it is a boy. Finally, it is
placed in the womb of its mother.

Sarakka – the 'splitting' or 'childbirth' grandmother and the goddess of fertility and menstruation – helps Sámi women through pregnancy and into childbirth. She lives in the central hearth of the house. A true empath, she is said to feel the pain with mothers as the births take place, and those mothers pay tribute by chopping wood during their labour. After the birth, the mother will eat special porridge named after Sarakka, sharing it with other women. Three wooden divination pegs are then put into the dish; in some areas one is white, one black and another has rings carved on it. The pegs are buried under the door after the birth: if the white one disappears, mother and child will be fine, but if the black one vanishes, the baby will not survive.

Juksakka – the 'bow' grandmother – lives at the back of the house, and protects the child in early infancy and teaches her to walk. In some places, a bow is placed in the post-birth porridge instead of pegs; the remains divine the fate of the child and are hung over its bed. The front of the house is the home of Uksakka – the 'door' grandmother – who also helps during labour and watches over the child as it grows and begins to walk. The Sámi keep her happy by pouring brandy on the ground by their front door.

A CIRCLE OF WOMEN

In an age when childbirth was an uncertain, even dangerous process, having a warm circle of women surrounding a young mother-to-be must have been of comfort and given her strength. In addition to the real-life village midwives and older women, these wise, benevolent spirits hovering in the background would give heart to a scared first-time birther. And the knowledge that they would be present beyond the delivery, creating a safe, warm space for the growing child would provide yet more reassurance. It might take a village to raise a child, but having some extra goddess hands would surely help.

But Madderakka isn't some dusty relic, confined to the past. In the seventeenth and eighteenth centuries, incoming Christians to the Sámi regions integrated her into their religion. The Bible's Mary, Mother of Christ, was known among the Sámi as Akka and, like her forebear, was called upon both in childbirth and to heal. Madderakka still remains popular in Sámi culture even to this day. She's evolved somewhat, now living under the floor of modern-age feminists' homes: she has become a totem for those seeking equal rights.

> 'Childbirth is more admirable than conquest, more amazing than self-defence, and as courageous as either one.'
> – GLORIA STEINEM

SARAKKA REBORN

In the 1970s, female Sámi reindeer herders started to demand parity. They'd been hit disproportionately by modernism – their traditional skills of skinning and homemaking were no longer needed to the same extent – and the increasing influence of Christianity meant that the very old, more matriarchal structure of their society was being eroded. In1988, they formed their own women's organisation, named after Sarakka, the beloved goddess of childbirth – an indication of the goddess' continuing importance and influence. In more recent years, yet more green shoots from older religions have peeped through. Sámi shamanism is undergoing a revival, through ceremonies, folk medicine and even in beauty salons that fuse ancient shamanistic healing with modern treatments. In the arts, contemporary Sámi artists such as Sofia Jannok, Elle Marja Eira and ice sculptor Elisabeth Kristensen nurture the memory of the spirit midwife who delivered generations before them, creating works inspired by their Sámi heritage.

Perhaps it's the earthiness of Madderakka and her family that appeals most. These women, entrusted with the most precious and arduous of tasks, to create new human life, are to be found living humbly in their believers' houses, under the floor, by the door, in the fire. Madderakka and her daughters are, thus, in every home – surrounding, nurturing, protecting. It's a comforting, close place for deities to exist – if you need them, even a whisper will bring them.

THE MOIRAI

GREEK:
INCARNATIONS
OF DESTINY

Also known as
The Fates
Moirae
Moerae

Often known as the Fates, these three incarnations of destiny control the lives of people and gods. Warping and wefting together, the Moirai spin a complex web of birth, life and death.

In Hesiod's *Theogony*, written c. 700 BCE, the Moirai are described as the daughters of Nyx, the mysterious, shadowy goddess of night, whose cloak swept over the sky and turned it black, and Erebus, a primordial deity who represented the deepest darkness. Even among the Greek pantheon, these gods were ancient, perhaps the last scraps of a Bronze Age Mycenaean religion.

Although Homer wrote about the Moirai in the singular in all but one instance, by the time Hesiod documented them in the eighth century BCE they had become three, each with an appropriate super heroine-like name. Clotho was known as The Spinner, producing the thread of life, which began when a mortal was born. She carried a spindle and governed the present. Lachesis was The Disposer of Lots. She measured the life thread, giving humans an element

'Your power extends to those
of mortal birth; to men with
hope elated, trifling, gay, a race
presumptuous, born but to decay.'
– ORPHIC HYMN 59 TO THE FATES

of luck and the opportunity to make what they could of their lives. She held a staff and governed the past. The small-but-terrifying Atropos was known as The Inevitable. This Morai held a pair of shears and governed the future. She cut a person's life thread at their death and represented the path of existence. The trio would appear three nights after the birth of every baby, to spin, measure and cut its particular filament, mapping life out from the very start. They were usually described as ancient crones, dressed in white, with tattered robes and with a cold demeanour, but sometimes depicted as hard-working younger women, with a more meticulous manner. As they appeared at birth, so they were present at marriages and also presided over death.

The Morai dictated the fate of everyone, rich or poor, good or evil, god or mortal. According to some second-century writers, including Hesiod and Greek Pausanias, Zeus had power over the trio, but others including Quintus Smyrnaeus told how even that mighty deity had to bow to these weavers of fortune. The Moirai were staunch allies of the king of gods and drove his bride, Themis, to their wedding. However, in later tales that sought to rework the stories from a more patriarchal perspective they were described as his daughters. They fought on his behalf in the battle between the Titans and the Olympians, and they used trickery to weaken his opponent, Typhon, with magical fruit.

Rather than taking a starring role in any one story, the Moirai were a brooding presence in the background of many myths, a glum chorus, reminding the actors, the gods and the readers of the prescribed nature of life and the grim inevitability of death. They spent some time in the Underworld with the Erinyes (the Furies, see pages 64–67) who would sometimes act as hired muscle for them, carrying out punishments. Plato describes them as sitting alongside the sirens, singing in harmony with those dangerous, alluring creatures and keeping the planets spinning, using the 'Spindle of Necessity'. The Underworld was also where the Moirai kept their records – every man's life, every event mapped out on tablets of brass and iron. They might have been dressed in rags and dishevelled, but they were meticulous administrators.

SISTERHOOD

The trio have sisters across the globe and time: the Norse Norns, Urðr (Wyrd), Verðandi and Skuld, who also use thread to map mortals' fates; the Valkyries (see pages 94–97), who worked a loom made from human remains to cast the fate of warriors; Mokosh, the slavic fertility goddess who weaves the threads of life, Mari (see pages 152–55), who threads the fate of her people, and the Celtic Matres, triplet goddesses. Their story also feeds into popular culture: Shakespeare's Macbeth has its three Weird Sisters, witches who foretell the future, and Allen Ginsberg tells of the 'three old shrews' in his poem 'Howl'.

The three women hold huge power in their hands and spindles. What bigger responsibility than to map out the destiny of all people, all gods, to be present at the birth and death of us all and keep the world running to plan. It's *almost* as if women are better at plate-spinning, multi-tasking and working as a team. These women have absolute power, but they wield it collaboratively, in harmony. Their unity and organisation keeps the complex system afloat. Or as Oprah Winfrey put it: 'When women put their heads together, powerful things can happen.'

BRIGID

Also known as
Brigit
Brig
Bride
Brigandu
Britannia
Mary of the Gael

She's been a saint for more than 1,500 years and a goddess long before that. She invented the personal attack alarm, lived as part of a lesbian couple and performed abortions. Goddess Brigid and her Christianised counterpart, St Brigid, represent the powerful feminine heartbeat at the core of Ireland.

In her goddess incarnation, Brigid came into this world as the sun crept into the firmament, rays beaming red and gold from her brow across the sky. A grand entry. Her name means 'bright arrow' or 'bright one'. In the *Lebor Gabála Érenn*, the book of Irish history written in the Middle Ages, she is described as the daughter of the Dagda – the father god of the supernatural tribe of deities, the Tuatha Dé Danann – and Boann, the goddess of fertility. A genetic combination of fierceness and artistic sensitivity defined this goddess of verse, healing, midwifery, blacksmithing, fire, spring and, most importantly, the sun.

In the Irish *Mythological Cycle*, a history of pre-Christian Ireland written in the Middle Ages, Brigid becomes the wife of Bres, king of the Fomorians, the

otherworldly race at war with the Tuatha Dé Danann. The eleventh- or twelfth-century reworking of the ninth-century *Cath Maige Tuireadh* (The Battle of Mag Tuired) tells how, on the death of her son Ruadan at the hands of the Tuatha Dé, she 'keened'. This was the first time this chilling cry was heard in Ireland, starting a tradition heard at gravesides until recent times and becoming the blueprint for the banshee's wail (see pages 126–29). In the same stanza, the writer tells how Brigid is best known for inventing a whistle for signalling at night – a proto-personal attack alarm, perhaps.

Brigid's influence flowed widely: she's Bride in Scotland, Brigandu in Brittany and Wales, Britannia in England and, in Vodou culture, the red-haired, white-faced, foul-mouthed, rum-drinking Maman Brigitte (see pages 214–17). She's often depicted as a triple goddess, sometimes as three sisters, maybe representing her patronage of poetry, healing or midwifery and smithing. All her personas have a fiery connection; the spark of inspiration for poetry, the hearthside for midwifery and the forge for smithing.

> 'I'd sit with the men, the women and God There by the lake of beer. We'd be drinking good health forever And every drop would be a prayer.'
> – SAINT BRIGID

Brigid has a particular connection with Imbolc, one of the quarterly Celtic fire festivals held on 1st February; it's a time to cherish the first green shoots coming from the ground, a whisper of the first stirrings of spring. It's also a deeply female celebration that anticipates the lambing season, the blossom, the deep breath before crops burst from the earth. There were, and still are, rituals to observe at this time, such as making a Brigid's cross from rushes – a four-legged representation of the sun, with a square at its centre – making a bed up for the goddess and the lighting of fires or candles. When the Christian church co-opted Brigid's festival and gave it a shiny rebrand, it kept the lamp-lighting element, renaming the new event Candlemas. But it wasn't just the goddess' day that the Church absorbed; it was Brigid herself.

FROM GODDESS TO SAINT

When Ireland was Christianised, around the fifth century, Brigid transformed from goddess to saint. Some believe the Christians transferred many of the goddess' traits to a real woman, St Brigid, others that St Brigid was a figure pulled together from the old tales. St Brigid's Day was now 1st February and the old traditions surrounding the festival were absorbed into the Christian celebrations. The all-new St Brigid had her own stories, which were just as incredible as the goddess with whom she was syncretised. There is much debate, but many believe she was born around 451 CE and that she led a life many in the modern Church would regard as unconventional. Reluctant to marry, one story tells how, rather than accept proposals, she asked God to take away her beauty, so he plucked out one of her eyes. To escape marriage permanently, she did as many women do, and became a nun – her eye miraculously returning as she took the veil. However, St Brigid was not without company; she had a female 'soul sister', Darlughdacha who shared her bed and became abbess of Kildare, the monastery that Brigid established on her friend's death. The saint died only a year after her beloved Darlughdacha.

Kildare was built over a shrine to Brigid's ancient goddess counterpart, but much older traditions were not entirely extinguished. The nineteen priestesses who had nurtured the deity's eternal flame were replaced by nineteen nuns who ensured the fire burned until Henry VIII had it snuffed out during the sixteenth-century English Reformation. Kildare was forward thinking, accepting both men and women to be monks and nuns. The inhabitants were culturally aware, keeping safe much ancient literature and learning during the purges of the Dark Ages.

St Brigid reportedly once fell asleep during one of St Patrick's notoriously interminable sermons. In another escapade, she was 'accidentally' ordained as a bishop by a priest. The Church later declared consecration was void, as the priest was in 'a holy trance'.

Brigid continued to act unconventionally. In 650 CE, the writer Cognitus described a miracle performed by the saint:

'A certain woman who had taken the vow of chastity fell, through youthful desire of pleasure and her womb swelled with child. Brigid, exercising the most potent strength of her ineffable faith, blessed her, causing the child to disappear, without coming to birth, and without pain. She faithfully returned the woman to health and to penance.'

So, compassionate doctor, iconoclast, equal rights advocate, lesbian, bishop, resister of a conventional lifestyles, it's *this* woman who is being reclaimed as an icon by modern women. In 1993, Brigid's sacred fire was relit by a group of Brigidine Sisters at a Christian centre for multi-faith spirituality in Kildare Town. The community of men and women who tend it are ardent advocates of reconciliation, peace and social justice.

At a time when abortion issues are at the forefront of the nation's minds, when the short fuse of sectarian violence dangles near the flame and when women's rights' demonstrations fill the streets of Dublin and Belfast, Brigid makes for a powerful role model in contemporary Ireland and beyond. You'll see her face on pro-choice group's banners on parades, her cross tattooed on shoulders. Even by contemporary standards, she's a radical, whose story has resonance worldwide.

ERZULIE DANTOR AND ERZULIE FREDA

VODOU: GODDESSES

Also known as
Ezilí Dantor
Erzulie D'en Tort and Lady Erzulie
Erzulie Fréda Dahomey

These contrasting Haitian love goddesses represent two very different kinds of women, one flirty and charming, the other steely and principled. One school of thought has the sisters as part of a triple deity with La Siréne, a goddess of the sea and a variation on Mami Wata. Others believe that the siblings are part of an even larger group of Erzulies, each representing a different aspect of the goddesses.

Vodou has two sets of *loas* (Haitian spirits) or gods: the Rada and Petro family. The Rada were the older pantheon of deities – ancestor and nature spirits – who boarded the eighteenth-century slave ships with the African people and endured the journey across the Atlantic to the plantations of Haiti, shoulder-to-shoulder with their worshippers.

The ceremonies, dances, trances and possessions that these people took from Africa into the New World helped them, to some extent, cope with the abuse they suffered at the plantations.

REVOLUTION AND RAGE

The Rada gods, in turn, were complemented by the Petro family, the newer, more aggressive *loas*, spawned from the unimaginably grim lives into which the slaves were thrust. As the Africans mixed with people from other countries, so they absorbed and adopted other religions' gods as Petro *loas*. The slaves even adopted some of the French Catholic icons of their 'masters'; they would sometimes use them as ciphers, substitutes for their original gods and goddesses, enabling them to continue to follow their old ways, hiding in plain sight. Eventually, these new icons become syncretised, absorbed into the Vodou religion.

The Polish Catholic Black Madonna was one of the icons adopted to mask a Vodou goddess. Her images were brought to Haiti by Polish mercenaries fighting in the late eighteenth-century Haitian revolution, which ended in victory and led to the independence of the colony. The Madonna was fused with Erzulie Dantor, one of the new Petro loas, taking on her dark skin and two facial scars. The uprising started after a feast honouring Dantor – and so she is credited with having started the war. Despite her goddess status, the islanders give her a place in real-life history, and thus it's told how she fought alongside the rebel slaves in the uprising, even enduring having her tongue cut out, an act that left her mute. She brought her raging temper and strength to the battle, her character forged in the conflict.

'And if you do not like me so, to hell, my love, with you.'
– DOROTHY PARKER

Dantor is a single mother, with a child, Anais. Some believe that this single motherhood was due to her being a lesbian and that she only slept with male gods in order to get pregnant; as a result she has been adopted as a patron saint of queer women – homosexuality is accepted in the Vodou religion. She is fiercely protective of women and children, particularly of those experiencing domestic violence and is seen as a champion of the disempowered. Unlike her emotional sister, Dantor doesn't weep; instead she channels her sadness into action and vengeance.

She is very much a goddess for real women, those struggling to keep their family afloat, those abused mentally and physically, those ostracised for their sexual choices. Her followers see in Dantor a reflection of their own tough lives. No wonder she is still fervently adored, worshipped and channelled into religious ceremonies today.

Contrasting with her fierce sister Dantor is Erzulie Freda, an African Rada *loa* and goddess of beauty, prosperity and dance. She wears three wedding rings, each a gift from one of her over-indulgent husbands, Ogun, Agwe and Damballah. She can almost be seen as a parody of a super feminine woman: she adores tiny sweets, diamond necklaces, white-frosted cakes and scented bubble baths. She will burst into a room in a puff of perfume, glass of pink champagne in hand, bubbles of laughter erupting, casting her eyes around for someone to seduce. And seduce them, she will. She's an equal opportunity lover: male or female, Freda doesn't care.

Lavish, generous with both money and affection, Freda loves to be flattered: tell her how beautiful she is, how good she smells and you'll have her attention. Once you have enraptured her, she will dance with you, erotically, closely, often uncomfortably so. However, men and women who have been close to Erzulie Freda – Vodou followers sometimes 'marry' her or are possessed by her spirit – describe the relationship as hollow and unfulfilling; she'll often cry, weeping because of the nature of love, that it must always end in sorrow. Her tears mirror those of her counterpart from Christian iconography, Our Lady of the Sorrows – the sobbing Virgin Mary. Freda is the guardian spirit of gay men, particularly drag queens, not surprisingly, as her appearance could almost be seen to resemble that of a drag artiste, serving pink realness. Men imitate her during Vodou ceremonies – acting coquettishly, dancing, but ultimately breaking down in tears.

The contrast between these two sister goddesses is striking: the honest, gruff, protective and strong Dantor and the softer, more capricious, almost spoiled Freda. Their very different attitudes towards love represent a wider dilemma many women face: to conform to the societal norms expected of women, whether you should smile at others, dance, flirt to get ahead – or to choose to be more Dantor and embrace your resting bitch face, retain integrity over expectation and to fiercely defend those who need it most.

Where do you fall?

BONA DEA

Also known as
Fauna
Feminea Dea
Sancta
Laudanda Dea

Cloaked in mystery, Bona Dea was a woman's woman – her rituals were carried out only by female initiates. Her intimate, heady ceremonies were rumoured to be laced with forbidden wine and lasted until dawn. Yet this female-centric millieu had a downside; as Bona Dea's existence was out of the sight of men, her story has been lost to many.

We can guess at some bare Bona facts; this matronly figure may have presided over fertility, virginity and healing – she was often portrayed carrying a snake, the symbol of medicine. This bears out the theory that her worship was merged with Greek healer goddess Damia, thought to be another name for Demeter. An alternative theory conflates her with either the wife or daughter of Faunus – the horned god of the forests and countryside.

Bona Dea had her own temple on the Aventine Hill in Rome, which is thought to have been built in the third century BCE. It was described as being a centre of healing, with its own herb stall and harmless snakes

'I've felt as if I didn't exist, as if I were
invisible, miles away from the world,
miles away. You can't imagine how
much alone I've been all my life.'
– IRIS MURDOCH, *THE SEA, THE SEA*

wandering its precincts. Designed with secret rooms and cubbyholes, the building was cared for and staffed exclusively by women and, unusually for a temple, had high walls. All this secrecy only served to intrigue Roman men, curious about what rites and riots went on within its boundaries.

And perhaps they had every right to suspect that worshipping this mysterious goddess was fun, as Bona Dea loved a festival. She had two, one in May, the other December. They were notable in being the only Roman festivals at which married women were allowed to gather together at night, drink strong wine and perform blood sacrifices. The May festival took place at the temple, attended by women from all walks of life, from slaves to those from higher classes.

The December event had a much more exclusive guest list, however. Held at the house of the Roman magistrate, but hosted by his wife, exactly what went on at this event was a matter of much speculation among the men of the city. We know that before the party started, the women attending took a temporary vow of celibacy and all representations of men were removed from the house, cloths hung over paintings and statues taken down. It was then decorated with flowers and a ritual feast prepared, accompanied by wine. Lots of strong, ceremonial wine. It was possibly as much social as religious – a chance to meet with other women with no men present, to catch up on gossip and to kick back in a woman-only space. The nobles danced to live music, made sacrifices and played games. The Roman writer Juvenal exclaimed: 'My god! Women get all stirred up with wine and wild music; they drive themselves crazy.' However, the women didn't refer to wine by name, and used the euphemism 'milk' instead.

This yearly party gained a different kind of notoriety in 62 BCE. The festival was being held at the home of Julius Caesar and hosted by his wife, Pompeia. In a strange plot twist, Caesar's political ally Pulcher dressed as a female harp player in order to gatecrash the ceremony and seduce his friend's wife. When he was discovered, the women were furious; not only had he been seeking to discredit Pompeia, but he'd also defiled their ceremony. There was an enormous scandal, which ended, in rather misogynistic fashion, in Clodius' acquittal and Caesar divorcing his wife who must always remain 'above suspicion'. This scandal tainted the December festival irreparably and it was cancelled. To be sure it was gone for good, the ceremony's name was run down, associated with scandal and bad behaviour. Even a hundred years later, Juvenal describes it as an excuse for women and men in drag to get drunk and cavort.

What went on behind the walls of Bona Dea's temple – and why – is a matter of speculation. Perhaps she was believed to help fertility, a taboo subject at the time, yet one that has been the source of fascination, shame and agony for women throughout history. Or perhaps the women of Rome needed a sanctuary, a healing, female-centred space where they could share knowledge, opinions and relax.

Alternatively, the fragile history of the goddess may just have been lost like dandelion seeds on the breeze – undocumented by male chroniclers. 'Women's interests' have historically been deemed unimportant – even today, many writers don't deem hard-hitting female-centric subjects such as childcare and the menopause as notable, let alone 'fluffier' topics such as fashion and make-up.

RECLAIMING HISTORY

In a perverse way, perhaps it's the erasure of Bona Dea from history that makes her so important. Maybe she represents the forgotten women; the innovators, great thinkers, artists and composers whose achievements have been sidelined or written out of history — women like Zelda Fitzgerald, whose quips husband F. Scott made a habit of 'borrowing', and people such as Chien-Shiung Wu, Lise Meitner and Jocelyn Bell Burnell, all overlooked for Nobel Prizes in favour of male counterparts working on the same projects – a phenomenon so common, it has a name, the Matilda Effect. Or Fanny Mendelssohn, sister of composer Felix, who remained stuck composing unpublished music at home in Berlin while her brother travelled the world, even garnering praise from Queen Victoria for one of his sisters' works. Like Bona Dea, the contribution of these women is sometimes impossible to quantify, but at least they are now starting to be recognised. How many other thousands, millions of women's efforts have been entirely lost to a male-scripted history?

Perhaps we should seize and elevate Bona Dea to be the symbolic patron of every silenced, overlooked woman. Maybe then her name might represent the hidden or lost contributions made by those sidelined over the years. And that by saying her name, by making Bona Dea part of the conversation, perhaps we are in some way reclaiming that history.

AME-NO-UZUME

JAPANESE: GODDESS

We all have that friend who can make us laugh until our sides hurt and tears stream down our faces. Someone who will go beyond the call of duty to make their friends giggle, whether that's telling a ridiculous joke, doing a spot-on impression of a boss or pretending to trip over. The story of Ame-no-Uzume, the Shinto goddess of dawn, mirth and revelry, shows that, even in ancient Japan, there was always someone who'd take pratfalling to a transcendental level.

Ame-no-Uzume's name translates as 'whirling' and she's the patron deity of dancers. She's also the goddess of good health – you might shake off aches and pains by drinking the water from her stream. She is effervescent, shining with vitality and good humour – the kind of woman you might find leaping and grinning at the front of a hot yoga class, pushing you on towards feats of achievement with a smile. Her followers are said to be blessed with long, happy lives, fuelled by her magic and so the goddess is often represented by aged wines or mature cheese. Alcohol, nibbles, dancing, hilarity,

essentially, everything you need for a great party, wrapped up in one woman – what's not to love?

AN EXTROVERT SAVES THE DAY

Ame-no-Uzume's outgoing personality was central to her crowning achievement: enticing the sun goddess Amaterasu out of hiding in a cave. This may sound like a small feat, but Amaterasu had fallen out with her brother, Susanoo. He'd been insulting her, squabbling over dares and challenges, then playing typical sibling pranks on her that included tearing down the fences of her rice fields. However, the annoying god went too far when he threw a flayed dead horse into his sister's weaving room, not just ruining her precious fabrics, but killing one of the workers, too. Furious, Amaterasu ran into a grotto and refused to come out. As she took the sun with her, the world was plunged into darkness.

Wily Ame-no-Uzume had an idea to lure out this deity the country relied on for light. She got an old bucket and a mirror and began to perform a strange dance outside of the grotto where the goddess hid. She climbed on top of the tub and arranged the glass so the gathered crowd of gods and goddesses could see up her skirt. Gasps followed – she wasn't wearing any underwear! The drumming of her feet still wasn't enough to pique the curiosity of Amaterasu, however, so Uzume went a step further and lifted up her long kimono, then, in a hilarious parody of a striptease, tore it open, baring her breasts. The deities all fell about laughing uproariously and the sound enticed the sulky sun goddess out from her hiding place. Some judiciously placed hay bales barred her way back into the cave, but they weren't needed for long; Amaterasu was so swept away by both her own shining reflection in the mirror and the revelry, she decided to stay outside – and so the sun was restored to the sky once again. The incident led to Ame-no-Uzume's nicknames as 'The Great Persuader' and 'Heavenly Alarming Female'. This craziness was no one-off – in a later story, she is said to have terrified a monster by exposing her breasts and laughing at the beast's reaction.

Ame-no-Uzume's lust for life and forthright nature are rare gifts in a goddess. Combined with her near-shamanistic ability to use dance as a cure-all, she becomes a triple threat. But she's not a grinning idiot – there is reason behind her behaviour: she uses her nakedness, her body, to disorientate. In revealing herself, she becomes vulnerable, yet laughs at the world and herself – a distracting political manoeuvre.

As a reward for her labours, she was made head of the Sarume Order of sacred dancers whose moves are said to have spawned kagura, the classical dance-mime still used in Shinto religious ceremonies. Her tub is further said to have inspired the rhythms of taiko drumming and there are percussion troupes named for her even today. Shamanic women who followed her, practising divination, were called 'Miko', a tradition that still endures, an unbroken ribbon to the present from ancient times. The importance afforded to Ame-no-Uzume by the ancient people of Japan reflects their respect for the divine feminine and the power of women.

Uzume is an earthly, earthy goddess; she's bawdy, charming, open-minded and without inhibition. She'll bring the enthusiasm, but will also include those who are left out, encouraging wallflowers to dance. She epitomises female energy, erotic ecstasy, abandon and unadulterated fun. A party girl, sure, but one with an enormous heart and strategic mind. A woman for us all to draw on in moments of insecurity – or just when we want to put a smile on the faces of our friends.

INANNA

MESOPOTAMIAN: GODDESS

Also known as
Ishtar
Athtar

Determinedly not a mother goddess, Inanna is
the epitome of an edgy, slightly scary girl – a
whip in one hand and a glass of champagne in
the other. Brave, selfish, demanding, but very
entertaining, she's the kind of woman whose
social media posts would fascinate, horrify and
always make headline news.

One of the oldest goddesses in the world – she has
been around for at least seven millennia, possibly more
– Inanna originated in Sumer, modern southern Iraq,
but her worship spread across Akkadia, Babylonia
and Assyria. She was later conflated with another
goddess, Ishtar (their names are used somewhat
interchangeably), and, some believe, with Venus and
Aphrodite. She was one of the most important deities
in the Mesopotamian mythos, representing war and
sexual love. As is the way with goddesses, some of her
attributes contradict each other – perhaps she was
an amalgam of earlier goddesses or possibly she was
the last of her pantheon to be created, 'mopping up'
the remaining patronages, prostitutes, rain, tavern,

Venus, fertility and fair play. She was sometimes portrayed with a beard to emphasise her masculine traits, with one foot on a lion, which represented her bravery.

Inanna was variously said to be the daughter of sky god An, of the moon god Nanna (Sin), Enlil or Enki. In her early incarnation in Sumerian poetry, she is depicted as a young girl, subservient to a patriarchal society. 'The Descent of Inanna', sometimes described as the world's first epic poem, was written somewhere between 3500 and 1900 BCE, possibly earlier. It tells the story of Inanna's trip to the Underworld to visit her recently widowed sister, Ereshkigal, Queen of the Dead. Accompanied by Ninshubur, her servant, Inanna dresses in her finest clothes and knocks at the door to the kingdom. However, her sister bolts the seven gates of the realm, only letting Inanna through if she takes off her crown, jewellery and one item of clothing at each door – perhaps to show that she is weapon free. Naked, she enters the throne room, where she is killed by the judges of the Underworld, her corpse hanged from a hook. A panicked Ninshubur goes to Inanna's father – in this story Enki – for help. Enki gives the servant two demons who return with Ninshubur to the Underworld, where they find Ereshkigal writhing in agony – as promised by Enki. They relieve her pain, but ask for Inanna's corpse in return. They receive it on the condition they find a replacement body to impale, to which they agree. Inanna's friends (including, quite endearingly, her beautician) are all in mourning, so are spared the grim fate of replacing her. However, on her return home, she springs back to life to find her husband Dumuzid lounging on her throne, entertaining some slave girls. Furious, Inanna sends him to take her place on the hook. This impulsive, somewhat callous move is typical of Inanna – she is careless with emotions and does exactly as she pleases, with little regard for consequences.

> 'Fickle, lascivious and cruel like Nature.'
> – SIMONE DE BEAUVOIR ON INANNA, *THE SECOND SEX*

A WOMAN OF MANY PARTS

This steely determination shines in other stories. It's believed that until the reign of King Hammurabi of Babylon, between 1792 and 1750 BCE, men and women were regarded as equals – Inanna represents this equality. An aggressive accumulator, she beats her father in a drinking contest and steals the 'meh' – rules for civilisation – thus becoming even more powerful. She is hilariously egotistical, once attacking a mountain and destroying it because she considers its very existence as a threat to her authority. She is violent and relentless in her pursuit of justice. After she is raped by Sukaletuda, the world's worst gardener, she pursues him doggedly, unleashing plagues of blood on the earth and flying in the sky 'like a rainbow' until she finds and kills him. In *The Epic of Gilgamesh*, written between 2700 and 1400 BCE, she furiously sends a bull to kill King

Gilgamesh when he refuses her advances: he rightly points out that all of her previous consorts have met a brutal end. These stories illustrate the goddess' bold assertion of feminine power, sexuality and aggression.

Inanna was bound tightly with sexuality, particularly sex outside marriage, and her worship reflected the goddess' untrammelled enthusiasm for the flesh. The 'sacred marriage' between the goddess and Dumuzid was celebrated and evoked in sexual ceremonies, where kings and priestesses would reenact the pair's union. Ishtar's priests were as unconventional as their goddess. During Sumerian times, her temples were populated by gala – priests who were male, but took female names, were androgynes or homosexual. Tranches of her followers also maintained that Inanna transformed men into women. Some scholars also believe that her worship included ritual fetishisation. It's said that, in order to please their dominatrix-archetype goddess, her followers would strip their clothes off, perform choreographed dances and writhe on the floor, coupling in an orgiastic frenzy. They would be whipped, the punishment only stopping when they screamed 'mercy' – perhaps the earliest example of a 'safe word'. Because of this extreme worship, some academics have proclaimed Inanna to be the first proponent of BDSM.

A CULTURAL GODDESS

Inanna's strength and unusual attributes have made her the object of fascination in culture both high and low. She appeared in books such as Leonidas Le Cenci Hamilton's 1884 narrative poem 'Ishtar and Izdubar' and even receives attention in the highly influential *The Second Sex* (1949), Simone de Beauvoir using Ishtar in an example of goddesses who have been ignored at the expense of male deities. It's her refusal to conform not just to society's expectations of women, but also that of gods, that marks her out as a true outsider. She has no interest in marriage, in family, in pleasing people or acting demurely. She's a fighter, aggressive and greedy for dominion. She's sexually assertive, demanding satisfaction and love and expects similar devotion from her followers, welcoming worship that teeters into insanity; perhaps the very definition of a cult leader.

There's also something childlike and gleeful about Inanna's manner; something hilariously spoiled in the way that she spares her friends, her servants and even her beautician from being hanged from a hook in eternal agony and chooses her cheating, lazy lover for that fate instead. She's like a larger-than-life entitled reality TV star – and it's kind of thrilling to see just how outrageous she can be.

MA'AT

EGYPTIAN: GODDESS

Also known as
Maat

The serene queen of multi-tasking, and quiet advocate for female equality, goddess Ma'at was the underrated workhorse of Egypt – without her, society would have descended into anarchy. Represented as a younger woman, proudly sporting the symbol of truth – an ostrich feather – on her head, Ma'at was the daughter of the sun god Ra, who spawned her through the magic of Heka; she was also the sidekick of Thoth, the god of wisdom. Ma'at represented the order that came out of chaos in the creation of the earth.

Egyptian women lived under the protection of a constellation of male and female deities, the pantheon of Egyptian goddesses reflecting the relative parity between the sexes. In the eyes of the law, women were allowed to own property, to drink alcohol, to serve on a jury, to choose their partner, marry for love and spell out their own pre-nuptial agreements. They worked – there were female doctors, even a small minority of priests and scribes. A few women – Hatshepsut, Nefertiti and Cleopatra – even reached the heights of pharaoh. This balance between the masculine and feminine was important; Egyptians placed huge store on harmony and cosmic order, and this concept was embodied by one of the more ancient of their goddesses, Ma'at.

CREATING ORDER FROM CHAOS

At the moment the world was created, Ma'at harnessed the shifting stars, seasons and actions of mortals, pulling them tightly into their place, setting their times and making sense of the universe. She created order from chaos. After the creation, she came to represent something a little more abstract, the principles of ma'at.

A set of forty-two rules that Egyptians were expected to live by, the principles covered family life, the wider community, the nation as a whole, the environment and the pantheon of gods. The Jewish and Christian Ten Commandments were thought to have been based on these principles, as well as the central tenets of Confuscianism and Taoism. The structure meted out appropriate punishments; a thief might have her hands cut off, a murderer might be executed. However, they also had more long-term reach in the afterlife.

Egyptians believed that, just after their death, they were judged. Would they make it to paradise? The Egyptian dead were embalmed, but their hearts were left in the body because they had to be weighed on scales against Ma'at's feather, which symbolically represented the forty-two laws of ma'at. The dead were required to declare the forty-two tenets, in front of the forty-two gods who represented them. Those who had behaved well went to live in The Field of Reeds – paradise – with Osiris, while Ma'at was believed to have her own section of paradise and to bless those who had lived within her principles. The news wasn't so good for those who hadn't lived by the laws, however. Their heavy hearts were eaten by Ammut, a god with the head of a crocodile, body of a lion and backside of a hippo.

Ma'at has neither the show-stopping magic and power of fellow Egyptian goddess Isis nor the slinky glamour of Bastet, her sisters who revel in modern attention. She only had one temple – at Karnak – erected in her honour. Yet she was a vital cog in the Egyptian deity system, creating and running smoothly the machine that keeps society on track, the framework and rules.

Like most women, her essential work was not high glamour or garlanded with awards, but hidden. Yet without her, Egyptian society would have descended into disorder and anarchy. She may have flown

'Few things are
brought to a successful
issue by impetuous desire,
but most by calm and
prudent forethought.'
– THUCYDIDES

relatively under the radar, but women in similar, unrewarded, roles are today seeking to be recognised.

In 2017, US journalist Gemma Hartley used the phrase 'emotional labour' to describe the 'life admin' that many women take on. Making travel arrangements, planning meals, sorting out school trip money, buying gifts or reminding their families of tasks they needed to perform – all tasks that are sometimes described by those on the other end of the request as nagging. It's unrewarded, obscured work that keeps families in order and on track, but leaves women exhausted and resentful, and it's often piled high onto those who already have day jobs. Scaling this principal up to Ma'at's level, keeping the universe in order must require an enormous amount of frantic, below-the-water-line paddling, yet Ma'at always looks serene.

In addition, her organisational skills defined Egyptian society and its principles of relative equality. Ma'at was supportive of her sisters, pushing for that parity, ensuring that their presence and effort was codified into law. Her powerful influence on both the legal system and social customs ensured that women were treated with respect, and allowed a degree of independence. You'll see traces of Ma'at in today's feminist lawyers – America's trailblazing fighter for gender equality Ruth Bader Ginsburg or champion of the underdog Gloria Allred. These women are focused, methodical, preferring to advocate their cause through quiet procedure rather than fighting on the streets. In this they draw on Ma'at, part activist, part lawmaker, with a very small ego – there was no limelight-seeking on her part. Her humility, work ethic and principled solidarity continue to inspire.

LIỄU HẠNH

VIETNAMESE: GODDESS

Also known as
Vân Cát
Giáng Tiên

The elevation of Princess Liễu Hạnh from historical figure to globally worshipped goddess epitomises the hunger for all women to have a role model who doesn't conform to societal norms. Her story also illustrates the need for every woman to have a cheerleader; in this case, a feminist writer who, when she retooled the princess' story, took the goddess from cult status to international superstar.

Thought to have emerged in the sixteenth century, Liễu Hạnh is one of the Four Immortals in Thanism, the indigenous religion of Vietnam, mainly practised across the Red River region and central to the mother goddess cult, Đạo Mẫu. Her worship, which involves spirit mediums, dances and trances, survived repression by the Communist regime and she is now more popular than ever.

The original Liễu Hạnh was said to have been based on a real-life person; variously a faithful daughter, a tavern owner, a market trader, even a prostitute. However, the eighteenth-century *Vân Cát Thần Nữ*

Truyện (The Story of the Vân Cát Goddess) contains the best-known version of the goddess' story. It was written by Đoàn Thị Điểm, unusually for the time, a female author. The capricious, artsy Princess Liễu Hạnh had many lives on earth, but her first, according to Thị Điểm, in 1557, started in dramatic fashion. Liễu Hạnh's father, Lé Thái Công, was pacing up and down, waiting for his overdue baby to be born. He was worried, as his pregnant wife was ill and no one seemed to be able to help. So when a man arrived at the gates of his village, claiming to have a cure, Thái Công was keen to let him in. Once the pair were alone, the man took out a gigantic jade hammer and smashed it into the ground, knocking Thái Công out cold.

VISIONS

As he lay unconscious, Công had a vision – he was inside the king of heaven, the Jade Emperor's palace, watching the emperor's princess daughter holding a delicate jade cup. She dropped and shattered it and was ordered from the palace by her furious father. Abruptly, Thái Công awoke to find that, while he was unconscious, his baby had been born. Heeding his vision, he named the child Giáng Tiên ('Descending Fairy') after the princess in the palace. His daughter grew up to be a good woman who loved poetry and singing. She married and had two children, but sadly, her perfect-sounding life was cut short – she died aged twenty-one.

'Her cult is considered a vital cog in the tourist industry, young people celebrating the goddess' shamanic, luck-giving powers, while drinking in the history of their country.'

On her death, Giáng Tiên ascended back into the heavenly palace: her father's vision hadn't just been a dream, and she wasn't a mortal but a deity! Her name was Princess Liễu Hạnh and she was the daughter of the Jade Emperor. However she missed her life on earth, so returned there, wandering the globe doling out punishments and blessings, and outliving her human family. She went on to have another child with a poor student, but again left her family for heaven, only to again become homesick for the mortal realm and return.

This time, she descended to the village of Vân Cát, along with two spirit friends, Que and Thi. There, she became a kind of chief; she blessed the good and punished the evil. Her following started to grow and the villagers built a temple to her. However, the ruling Cảnh Tri dynasty regarded her as an evil influence, and so used its armies and magicians to destroy her church. Shortly afterwards a mysterious plague destroyed all the area's animals (massive side-eye thrown in Liễu Hạnh's direction). Luckily, the Princess was on hand to restore the livestock, on condition that her temple was rebuilt. The terrified dynasty not only quickly restored the temple, but in terrified overdrive, declared the princess 'supernatural and extraordinary' and gave her a new title: Mã Hoàng

Công Chúa (Golden Princess to Whom Sacrifices Are Made as to the God of the War). Liễu Hạnh worship was incorporated into Đạo Mẫu, a mother goddess religion, which venerates female figures. This religion is thought to have been popularised by the wealthy female traders of the area's markets – places that predominantly served soldiers – and it's the nature of these worshippers that perhaps gives a clue to the real-life origins of Liễu Hạnh.

It's thought that writer Đoàn Thị Điểm's documentation of these stories reflected her own passions and life. She was an ardent feminist and portrayed the princess as a woman who liked to challenge men intellectually and chose her own path. The writer also cleverly cherry-picked elements of the Taoist and Buddhist religions. Her tales form the basis of modern Liễu Hạnh worship.

RESONATING WITH THE MODERN WORLD

Both the rewritten stories and the Đạo Mẫu religion resonated with ordinary, working-class women (and men). Lên đồng was, and still is, among its practices. This form of worship sees spirit mediums go into trances, invoked by song, dance, costumes and particularly music. Followers give offerings that now include cigarettes and paper representations of worldly goods, from flat-screen televisions to designer handbags. Banned (fairly unsuccessfully) under successive dynasties from the late-seventeenth century, the religion was totally outlawed in 1945 by early Communist leaders who saw it as superstitious, old-fashioned nonsense. However, the cult merely went underground with people worshipping at private altars in their homes and holding secret séances. In the late 1980s, Communist rulers realised the power of a country's cultural history to bond and inspire its people. Rules were relaxed, and Liễu Hạnh was back! Today her cult is considered a vital cog in the tourist industry, young people celebrating the goddess' shamanic, luck-giving powers while drinking in the history of their country. Her fame has spread into the wider Viet diaspora, ceremonies regularly taking place in the US, Italy and Australia. Millions now celebrate the anniversary of the Mother Goddess' death which takes place during the third lunar month.

Liễu Hạnh took a fascinating path to goddesshood, a historical figure conflated with myth, who appealed predominantly to women and who became embedded in religious culture, thanks to their tenacious worship. Her tale may have been bolstered by a feminist writer with an agenda, but it is still little wonder that Liễu Hạnh is so wildly popular.

MAMAN BRIGITTE

VODOU: GODDESS

Also known as
Gran Brigitte
Grann Brigitte
Manman
Manman Brigit

If you're looking for a floaty, dreamy, winsome goddess, flip the page. This sexy Vodou icon dances the banda like nobody's watching, drinks rum infused with hot peppers and swears like a brigand. Bad girls with a good heart will find inspiration in Maman Brigitte.

Maman Brigitte and husband Baron Samedi are Vodou death *loas* – you'll find them swaying through the cemeteries and bars of Haiti and the southern states of America. The first gravestone in a Haitian burial ground is ceremonially carved with a cross and belongs to Brigitte, who protects tombs and graves marked in this way.

These guardians of the dead have a strong look. They dress steampunk-style – she favours a low-cut Victorian-style, black-and-purple dress and veil, he sports a distinctive top hat, frock coat and dark glasses, his neck hung with heavy jewellery and crosses and his face painted like a skull. They share bottles of spicy rum and both have potty mouths, swearing, telling dirty jokes and cackling. In short, they sound like a lot of fun.

Brigitte's copper-red hair, green eyes and pale skin mark her out as one of the very few white *loas*. Her looks are thanks to her Irish roots and her ancestor, Brigid (see pages 186–89). Most other *loas'* origins are in the gods of the African slaves or were created by syncretising black icons from other religions into the Vodou religion (see Erzulie Dantor and Erzulie Freda for more about the *loa* system, page 190–93), but Maman Brigitte came to the plantations via a different route; in the hearts and pockets of women shipped over from Ireland and Scotland in the eighteenth and nineteenth centuries. They were sent as indentured labour (a form of slavery) or as punishment for 'prostitution' – which at that time could be defined as becoming pregnant through rape or holding hands with a boy. These young girls brought with them 'Bridie dolls' – tiny poppet representations of their countries' beloved St Brigid to comfort them on their long voyage into the unknown, and which were believed to be the forebears of the Vodou doll. As the girls mingled with the slaves and workers shipped over from Africa, so Brigid was absorbed into the pantheon of Vodou *loas* as the mother of the Ghede family, the group of ancestral spirits that stand somewhere between the traditional African Rada pantheon of deities and the new Petro *loa*, formed in the crucible of the slaves' new life on the plantations.

WHITE SWAN TO BLACK ROOSTER

Like many of the women who brought her over, in order to survive in her new home, Brigid had to pull on a tougher, darker mantle. Her white swan symbol transformed into a black rooster, her affection for weavers transferred to gamblers and her chastity flipped into an ability to dance the banda in a sexy fashion and make lewd double entendres. However, many similarities remain: her crosses, still fashioned from rushes in Ireland, have echoes in her gravestone symbols; fire is still an important part of her worship and her festival is still celebrated at the start of February, at Imbolc.

She does have a caring, practical side. A healer, called upon when one of her followers is chronically ill or in need of a radical cure, she sometimes has to make the tough decision to let those people die, leading them tenderly to their life beyond the grave. She also reclaims the souls of the recently dead, transforming them into members of her gleefully decadent Ghede family. This group of souls seems to have a ball, drinking, having sex, dancing and cursing. They're dead so there is no retribution for bad behaviour and shame is non-existent. They make death seem like a never-ending party, a party where she is the drunken, grinning host.

In Western society, mortality is taboo, spoken of in whispers in antiseptic corridors or hidden behind heavy hospice doors. Undertakers cloak death in euphemisms as coffins make their final trip behind polyester curtains. Brigitte's 'tell it like it is' manner is a refreshing change – she has no time for fools in this world or the next. She is straightforward, yet empathetic, bridging the gap between life and death. She lives in graveyard liminality, ushering souls to the next world, while remembering and naming ancestors; looking forward and back at the same time. She may look intimidating, she may behave in a coarse fashion, but she is deeply compassionate and has a good heart, reminding us that sometimes good girls don't wear white.

Such a distinctive appearance and attitude makes Brigitte and her Baron beau popular characters in TV series, films and video games. Her husband's appearance astride a train in Bond novel and film, *Live and Let Die*, is iconic; he appears in Graham Greene's *The Comedians* and his villainous lookalike, Doctor Facilier, even pops up in Disney film *The Princess and the Frog*. Maman is also drawn upon by artists; most notably, Beyoncé channelled her in the video for 'Formation', filmed in post-Katrina New Orleans.

However, it's surprising that Maman Brigitte isn't even more popular as an icon. She's that rare beast, a goddess who is more mortal than most earth-bound humans. Her uninhibited behaviour is a stark contrast to antecedent Brigid's virginal demeanour. The thought of the duo out together is fascinating. What a pair the two would make – innocent Brigid seduced by the lights and music of the place, her sister guide leading her deeper into its dark recesses, dancing together – contrasting yin and yang of the same, compassionate, guiding goddess and whirling and blurring together until they are indistinguishable.

GLOSSARY

Chthonic
The gods of the Underworld. Used mainly in relation to the beliefs of the ancient Greeks. See: Hecate

Creolisation
The mixing together of people and cultures to become one. Originally a Caribbean concept, where it was used from the sixteenth century to describe the intermingling of people from different countries, religions and backgrounds due to the slave trade. Many popular religions in Haiti, Cuba, Trinidad and Brazil are described as Creole – a mixture of African and European symbols, tenets and ceremonies. See: Mami Wata

Crossroads
A place where two paths cross, believed across many cultures worldwide to be a space where the boundary between the spiritual and earthly world is at its thinnest. The veil becomes even thinner at sunset and sunrise, or as the season turns. Many cultures believe them to be unlucky places where evil lurks. See: Hecate; The Cihuateteo; La Llorona

Goddess movement
A rise in religious interest and analysis paralleled the rise of feminism. Some women (and men) chose – and still choose – to rekindle ancient goddess religions, now known under the broad term of the Goddess movement.

Great Goddess
Some historians believe that, prior to the Abrahamic God associated with much of Western religion, a single mother goddess, representing fertility, creation and the earth was worshipped across the Mediterranean, Europe, the Near East, much of Russia, North Africa, India and part of China. Other writers maintain that this theory is flawed.

Psychopomp
A creature, spirit or deity whose task is to accompany newly dead souls from earth to the afterlife. See: Berchta; Morrígan

Sacred Feminine, the
The concept that gods and human consciousness are neither male nor female, but rather a balanced essence of the two, interdependent,

symbolised by the yin and yang. The sacred (or divine) feminine is the aspect associated with traditionally female traits – creation, intuition, community, sensuality and collaboration.

Syncretism
The merging, or the attempted merging, of religions, sometimes resulting in a new belief system. Commonly occurs when people of one faith are conquered by another and their ideas are subsumed into the dominant religion, but not completely eradicated. See: Erzulie Dantor and Erzulie Freda; Maman Brigitte

Triple-aspect goddess
A deity believed to have three component figures, and found in cultures across the world. Often described as 'maiden', 'mother' and 'crone', the three aspects are believed to represent the waxing and waning of the year, the phases of the moon and, more literally, a woman's life cycle. See: Morgan Le Fay; Berchta; Hel; Mari

Tuatha Dé Danann
The supernatural race at the core of Irish mythology, endowed with special powers. Many believe them to be the gods and goddesses originally worshipped in the country, subsumed into fairy tale by Christian writers. See: The Banshee; Brigid

Wild Hunt
A story common to folklore across Europe, the Wild Hunt was said to gallop across the sky. In Norse culture, Odin would head a band of spirits of fallen warriors, in Germany, Berchta led the charge of a motley crew of ghosts, wild creatures and dogs, while in England, Herne the Hunter stampeded through Richmond Park. The hunt is closely connected to winter, to the dead, and the Underworld. See: Berchta

Yōkai
The Japanese pantheon of ghosts, monsters and demons. Not necessarily malevolent, they come in the shape of animals, humans or inanimate objects. See: Futakuchi-onna

FURTHER READING

Folklore, Myths and Legends of Britain, Russell Ashe, Kathleen Biggs, et al. Reader's Digest, 1973.

From The Beast To The Blonde: On Fairy Tales and Their Tellers, Marina Warner. Vintage, 1995.

A Dictionary of Fairies, Katharine Briggs. Penguin, 1976.

The World of the Unknown: Ghosts. Usborne, 1977.

The Book of English Magic, Philip Carr-Gomm and Richard Heygate. Hodder Paperbacks, 2010.

Absolute Sandman, Vols 1–4, Neil Gaiman. DC Comics, 2011.

Jonathan Strange and Mr Norrell, Susanna Clarke. Bloomsbury, 2004.

Women Who Run With The Wolves: Contacting the Power of the Wild Woman, Clarissa Pinkola Estés. Rider, 1993.

The Viking Spirit, Daniel McCoy. CreateSpace Independent Publishing Platform, 2016.

Breaking the Mother Goose Code: How a Fairy-Tale Character Fooled the World, Jeri Studebaker. Moon, 2015.

Dictionary of Celtic Mythology, James MacKillop. Oxford University Press, 2004.

Afrofuturism: The World of Black Sci-Fi and Fantasy Culture, Ytasha Womack. Chicago Review Press, 2013.

Yokai Attack!, Hiroko Yoda and Matt Alt. Kodansha International, 2008.

The Faces of the Goddess, Lotte Motz. Oxford University Press, 1997.

The Myth of Matriarchal Prehistory, Cynthia Eller. Beacon Press, 2001.

'Death and the Divine: The Cihuateteo, Goddesses in the Mesoamerican' Cosmovision, Anne Key. PhD diss., California Institute of Integral Studies, 2005.

Cult, Culture, and Authority: Princess Lieu Hanh in Vietnamese History, Olga Dror. University Of Hawaii Press, 2007.

Surviving Slavery in the British Caribbean, Randy M. Browne. University Of Pennsylvania Press, 2017.

Through the Earth Darkly: Female Spirituality in Comparative Perspective, Jordan Paper, Bloomsbury, 2016.

Nordic Religions in the Viking Age, Thomas DuBois. University of Pennsylvania Press, 1999.

Mother Russia: the Feminine Myth in Russian Culture, Joanna Hubbs. Bloomington: Indiana University Press, 1993.

Mermaids: The Myths, Legends, and Lore, Skye Alexander. Adams Media, 2012.

Lives of the Necromancers: or, An account of the most eminent persons in successive ages, who have claimed for themselves, or to whom has been imputed by others, the exercise of magical power, William Godwin, 1756–1836.

New Perspectives on the History and Historiography of Southeast Asia, Michael Arthur Aung-Thwin and Kenneth R. Hall. Routledge, 2011.

The Madness of Epic: Reading Insanity from Homer to Statius, Debra Hershkowitz. OUP Oxford, 1998.

The Devil: Perceptions of Evil from Antiquity to Primitive Christianity, Jeffrey Burton Russell. Cornell University Press, 1987

Jezebel: The Untold Story of the Bible's Harlot Queen, Lesley Hazleton. Doubleday 2009.

Quotes taken from:

The Acts of King Arthur and his Noble Knights, John Steinbeck, Penguin UK, 2001

Circe, Madeleine Miller, Bloomsbury Publishing, 2019

Baba Yaga's Assistant, Candlewick Press, Marika McCoola, 2015

We Should All Be Feminists, Chimamanda Ngozi Adichie, HarperCollins UK, 2014

Jane Eyre, Charlotte Brontë, Wordsworth Classics, 1847

Farewell, My Lovely, Raymond Chandler, Penguin, 1940

Women Who Run With the Wolves: Myths and Stories of the Wild Woman Archetype, Clarissa Pinkola Estés, Rider, 1996

East of Eden, John Steinbeck, Penguin Classics, 1952

The Four-Chambered Heart, Anaïs Nin, Duell, Sloan and Pearce, 1950

Cleopatra: A Life, Stacy Schiff, Virgin Books, 2011

Outrageous Acts and Everyday Rebellions, Gloria Steinem, Open Road Media, 2012

The Sea, The Sea, Iris Murdoch, Chatto & Windus, 1978

The Second Sex, Simone De Beauvoir, Penguin, 1949

MYTHOLOGICAL WOMEN PLAYLIST

Music is referenced throughout the book. This playlist features songs mentioned directly, songs that inspire me, as well as some more goddess, spirit and monster tunes. Go to:
tinyurl.com/mythologicalwomen

1. 'The Witch', The Rattles
2. 'Isis', Bob Dylan
3. 'Abre Camino', Death Valley Girls
4. 'Rhiannon', Fleetwood Mac
5. 'Isis', Yeah, Yeah, Yeahs
6. 'Má vlast (My Country): No. 3', Šárka', Bedřich Smetana
7. 'Venus', Shocking Blue
8. 'Awful Sound (Oh Eurydice)', Arcade Fire
9. 'Persephone', Cocteau Twins
10. 'Caught a Lite Sneeze', Tori Amos
11. 'Aurora', Björk
12. 'La Llorona', Lila Downs
13. 'Agamemnon', Violent Femmes
14. 'Silkie', Joan Baez
15. 'Calypso', Suzanna Vega
16. 'Scheherazade op 35 The Festival of Baghdad', Rimsky-Korsakov
17. 'Venus as A Boy', Björk
18. 'Jezebel', Frankie Laine
19. 'The White Hare', Seth Lakeman
20. 'Pandora's Golden Heebie Jeebies', The Association
21. 'Jezebel', Dizzee Rascal
22. 'Blind Goddess of the Nine Plagues', Loviatar
23. 'Black Forest (Lorelei)', Mercury Rev
24. 'Pandora's Box', Procul Harum
25. 'Cihuateteo', Bird Eater

ACKNOWLEDGEMENTS

This book is for my mum and dad.

Love to: Jeff, Dusty and Arthur.

Huge thanks go to: Aruna Vasudevan for her cheerleading, support, hard work and meticulous editing skills. Harriet Lee Merrion for her beautiful, sensitive illustrations that brought the book alive. Philippa Wilkinson at White Lion for believing in the idea and setting me on the right path. Julia Shone, Emma Harverson and Paileen Currie also at White Lion. Juliet Pickering and Hattie Grünewald at Blake Friedmann for superior agenting. Resham Naqvi and Daisy Way at Blake Friedmann for their ninja nitty-gritty skills. Guri and Elisabeth for Scandinavian and Sami intel. Esther Brownsmith at Mostly Dead Languages for her Baal Cycle translations. Christina Griffiths for the MacBook.

KATE HODGES is a journalist and writer. She was the front section editor of *The Face*, deputy editor of *Bizarre Magazine* and has worked on staff for *Just Seventeen*, *Smash Hits*, *The Green Parent* and *Sky Magazine* as well as for Rapido TV, makers of *Eurotrash*. Her books include *Little London* (2014), *London in an Hour* (2016), *Rural London* (2017) and *I Know a Woman* (2018). She is a musician, in cult bands *Ye Nuns* and *The Hare and Hoofe*. She lives in St Leonards-on-Sea with her two children, Arthur and Dusty.

HARRIET LEE-MERRION is an award-winning illustrator based in Bristol, in the South West of England. Her work has been published worldwide and exhibited internationally in New York, London and Berlin. She has illustrated for numerous clients including The British Library, Conde Nast, *The Guardian*, *The Washington Post* and *The New York Times*.

Quarto

First published in 2020 by White Lion Publishing,
an imprint of The Quarto Group.
One Triptych Place, London
SE1 9SH, United Kingdom
T (0)20 7700 6700
www.Quarto.com

Text © 2020 Kate Hodges
Illustrations © 2020 Harriet Lee-Merion

A catalogue record for this book is available from the British Library.

ISBN 978 1 78131 926 0
Ebook ISBN 978 1 78131 927 7

10 9 8 7 6 5 4

Design by Paileen Currie

Printed in Malaysia